PUBLIC SPEAKING

The authors, Dennis Castle and John Wade have known each other for over twenty years, appearing on bills together and even replying to each other in after-dinner speeches. They have previously collaborated on stage and radio scripts.

Dennis Castle made his first public speech at 16 in the Connaught Rooms and has since been constantly in demand as an after-dinner speaker. He was a compère and jack-of-all-trades speaker at the London Press Club's famous dinners for thirty years. He is also a professional actor on television, novelist, writer and journalist.

John Wade regularly makes after-dinner speeches internationally and has been to New York many times presenting his cabaret. He is a compère introducing international headline stars on tours throughout the United Kingdom, South Africa, Europe; the United States and Russia. As a Member of the Inner Magic Circle he is a popular and amusing lecturer and writer – at home, on television and abroad – speaking about the history of magic, magicians and the Magic Circle.

PUBLIC SPEAKING

Dennis Castle and John Wade

TEACH YOURSELF BOOKS
Hodder and Stoughton

First published 1980
Seventh impression 1990

ISBN 0 340 32160 1

Printed and Bound in Great Britain for
Hodder and Stoughton Educational,
a division of Hodder and Stoughton Ltd,
Mill Road, Dunton Green, Sevenoaks, Kent,
by Clays Ltd, St Ives plc

Contents

To
Paddy and Dabber Davis
*with the authors' admiration
and esteem*

Acknowledgements

We, the authors, wish to thank Roy Plomley OBE for his generous Foreword and taking so much trouble on behalf of this book. We are grateful to Anthony (Dabber) Davis and his wife Paddy of Associated Speakers for 'loaning' us their vast backstage experience in the world of public speaking. We are also indebted to Ruth Kimber, Sheila Souter, Marie Castle, Lydia Greeves and Barbara Moles for their help in their various roles in the process of turning the manuscript into print. In public speaking you need critical friends and we count ourselves lucky in having them.

D.C. J.W.

Foreword

This is a clear, complete and excellent book. Public speaking is not difficult, if you know how to set about it, and to learn not only its basic techniques but also its subtleties you could not be in better hands than those of Dennis Castle and John Wade.

While, in general, the standards of the mass-produced things of life have sunk lamentably low, the standards of individual *expertise*, from brain surgery to running a mile, have grown better and better – and this certainly applies to public speaking. There was a time when a speaker, delighting in the sound of his own voice, could get away with a large percentage of useless rhetoric, and his listeners would accept boredom as an inevitable part of speechmaking – but not any more. With television and radio in every home, people know how words can be used amusingly and informatively, and they will not accept empty phrasing or careless delivery.

It is good that our authors belong to different generations, because the ground they cover is that much greater. Dennis Castle began speaking as a law student before the war, and continued as a lecturer while in the Indian Army, where he was called upon to deal with subjects far removed from military matters, and to speak at several Indian universities and colleges. He is an actor and entertainer, a novelist and a writer of instructional books; and thus has been dealing with words all his working life. I have heard him speak many times, and always with great pleasure.

John Wade is a conjuror, and his ability has been recognised by the award of his profession's highest accolade, membership of the Inner Magic Circle. It is said that in conjuring the quickness of the hand deceives the eye, and in John's case the quickness of the tongue helps too, because his patter, mainly extempore, is a delight. He now lectures on his subject, and has toured Europe, South Africa, the United States of America, and Russia. He is also the author of a successful book, *The Trade of the Tricks*.

Both have appeared many times, and in several countries, on radio and television; John Wade as BBC commentator on current affairs, and Dennis Castle as a deft interviewer. Both, too, have been on the receiving end in interviews, which can be an art in itself and which this book covers. They are greatly in demand as after-dinner speakers, and have become experts in sensing audience reaction, never taking any gathering for granted. One thing they have in common is a quiet delivery – yet never a word is lost – and they know how to 'time' their words to gain the utmost effect.

Public Speaking will provide information and reassurance for the beginner, the means of a fresh start for those who have failed in the past for want of such information and reassurance, and a reminder of many tricks of the trade for the experienced. Whether you choose public speaking as a hobby or to assist you in your career – and to be able to think on your feet is an invaluable asset – you will find all you need to know in these pages.

There is more to public speaking than the speech itself : there is stage management, there is planning, there is conquering nervousness, and there is the ability to cope with emergencies, both major and minor; I have never before seen all these important facets dealt with in print. As a self-taught public speaker, I only wish I had had this book to guide me through my early days of trial and error.

Roy Plomley

1

Initial Observations on Resourceful Speaking

The greater the man, the simpler his speech. That is why he is great – more people have been able to understand his messages.

Successful public speaking means holding an audience's interest while imparting information. It is a form of salesmanship in which the vendor has to be careful to make his product really appealing rather than create suspicion by over-selling himself.

Public speaking should not be considered a formal ritual (although some die-hards in the Victorian tradition would have it so) but a platform for naturalness and the passing on of knowledge and instruction with clarity. People who find the thought of public speaking daunting are often those who have been subjected to heavy oratory rather than down-to-earth, concise phrasing. Fortunately more progressive education is erasing that. The modern world has little time now for mere flowery eloquence. It wants facts, easily-comprehended guidance and will not be bored by superficial outpourings.

How can speaking in public help you? You may have many reasons for wanting to master this accomplishment, but we have found that its overall value today lies in people's careers. Commerce, now, sets great store by public appearance. It has become a viable qualification for jobs. Yet once upon a time appearing before audiences was never considered either necessary or possible in most forms of employment. All that has changed. Today the man or woman able to stand up before a crowded room to say their piece is in great demand.

Many readers will have found themselves suddenly dragged

from their desk, work bench or laboratory to address a sales meeting or inter-office conference to make a verbal report on their link with it. If little or no notice has been given, it can, at first, be an unnerving moment especially if they have to follow more experienced speakers. But rise they must because their careers and promotion may well depend on their ability to present facts in concise language. They may never seek other forms of public speaking but work seminars will still require them to have a sound knowledge of it.

Other readers in less demanding professions may see public speaking as a social asset, proposing toasts at dinners or enthralling luncheon clubs with their experiences. Public speaking takes many forms from the lecture-hall to light-hearted social discourse, the instructional talk to a specialised audience or the tensions of the political platform. But however you approach the art, whether as a professional necessity or a diverting hobby, the ability to speak before an audience will play a key role in your life. You will have the authority to command attention, and thereby become a force to reckon with.

Before we analyse all the various aspects, however, there is always the first bridge to cross, the question that arises in every future public speaker's mind: 'Have I really got the nerve to face audiences?'

Of all human fears, that of making a fool of oneself in public is the greatest. It can date back to our first nervous day at school when already established pupils summed us up as, haltingly, we spoke our first words aloud in the classroom – our name! With everyone looking at us, everyone listening to us, even our name sounded absurd. But that feeling of inadequacy, of stage-fright, is suffered by all professionals taking the first steps in their careers. Actors brood on forgetting lines, singers and musicians dread hitting wrong notes, school teachers or instructors fear having facts disproved in their very first lesson by mocking pupils, athletes panic at the thought of dropping the baton ... all shudder at the thought of abject failure before a derisive crowd.

Yet, although everyone suffers these dark moments in their

minds, in reality they rarely experience much beyond a rather embarrassing *faux pas* in company which is almost always covered by an apology. But the sensation of ridicule remains.

However, you can take heart. Such sensitivity proves that you are aware of your own fallibility and initial limitations. This acknowledgement is your strongest asset in becoming a successful public speaker. By considering your weaknesses at the onset you are seeking perfection. No one can start with a better approach. You are being sincere with yourself, the first qualification a good speaker needs.

The brash, over-confident, self-important, 'I never suffer from nerves' individual recalls the young actress who, when coming off the stage from saying her two lines, saw the great Sarah Bernhardt shaking anxiously in the wings before her big entrance. 'You are nervous, madame?' cooed the girl, 'Me – I never suffer from nerves on the stage.' The Divine Sarah replied: 'Ah, my child, but you will – when you have some talent. . . .'

Those who think they know it all without training, who would run before they walk, make more public speaking gaffes in a month than you will ever make in a lifetime. Possessed of a superiority complex they will never remain content to learn by the trials which reduce error and soon find themselves struck off speaking lists. Audiences just will not put up with unstructured speeches.

Public speaking demands discipline. Like the good athlete you must know your best distances and train for them so that, as you gain confidence and experience, you can extend on your already proven strengths. Mistakes are only made if we have not kept ourselves aware of the hazards that can baulk us in the first place. So you must develop a keen sense of proportion in respect of your abilities.

Vanity is the self-destructor of a public speaker. There is a vast difference between having full and justified confidence in yourself and what you say, and an inflated ego. Once the audience senses pomposity or intolerance they bridle and are less receptive. And, at the other end of the scale, a limp, flat-voiced speaker who gabbles, perhaps inaudibly, to get his speech over and done with will also annoy an audience because he not only bores them but denies them the facts they came to hear.

But vanity must not be confused with ambition. The true desire to succeed on public platforms is commendable and it will only be jealous second-raters who, purposely, equate ambition with self-aggrandisement to disparage a more successful rival.

Speakers *must* respect their audiences. A hint of superiority and they will withdraw their enthusiasm. The 'power' you must achieve is presenting your facts in an 'entertaining' manner. By 'entertaining' we do not mean necessarily raising laughs, although if humour is used correctly within the context of your theme and the occasion it is a very strong reinforcement. 'Entertaining' in public speaking means keeping your audience in a relaxed affable mood through your talk so that they absorb your points happily and eagerly. But, tauten them with hard-to-fathom irrelevancies, or long, dull diatribes and you will lose their full attention. Attempts to infuse comedy when not appropriate inevitably spell trouble. Apposite humour is, of course, a sure ally as it is safe to say that a laughing audience obviously cannot be bored!

Public speaking has been defined many ways, the most succinct being the earliest known reference by Aristotle in his 'Writings on Rhetoric' around 315 BC. Public speaking, he said, was 'The Art of Persuasion' which practically covers every aspect – but not quite. There are cold, hard facts, historical occurrences and logical progressions on which an audience does not need to be 'persuaded' to accept. But in their application to your subject perhaps you may have to 'persuade' the audience that they are relevant. Public speaking cannot really be over simplified under one heading. After all 'persuasion' can be a form of 'indoctrination' ... a sinister application doubtless used in Aristotle's time! We prefer to call public speaking 'commentary on the occasion' bearing in mind each function at which a speaker rises to address an audience varies considerably in essence every time he is engaged.

Public speaking is not an inherited gift, although perhaps a conducive environment as a child helps considerably. A good home, understanding parents, scholastic encouragement and plenty of conversation will equip a girl or boy to face audiences more confidently than the unfortunate loners who have been denied much dialogue. But the latter, if they make the grade on public platforms, often have the more valuable story to tell! Hard won experience is a vital ingredient in many forms of public speaking.

Ultimately good public speaking is the result of diligence – and being a good listener!

The art of conversation

To be really outstanding in public speaking you must be able to converse with other people. Conversation in general terms is limited since so many other forms of communication have replaced it. Nobody wants you to chat while they are watching television or listening to the radio. And, perhaps because of the rise in street crime figures, amicable conversations between passers-by have decreased. Ask a stranger today the way and he may first treat you with suspicion, even querying your reason for wanting such directions in the first place!

It is a sad indictment of the times that neighbourly chats over garden walls are rare now. Flat dwelling has cut people off, family by family, and now they only pass the time of day in lifts and corridors. The loss of gardens, vegetable patches and back porches are, like the demolition of theatres, sites of entertainment gone forever. Inns and hotels have disco music now and those who want to talk at a bar have to shout above a din. So vocabulary recedes into basic, monosyllabic phrases. It is harder to learn from our neighbours now. The invaluable exchange of experience, which is meat and drink to a public speaker, is not so easy to come by as progress seems to create more loneliness.

But, like these changes or not, we are stuck with them and they have to be taken into account when you enter public speaking. 'Modern' pressures are blamed for much frustration. Leisure time hangs heavily upon some who are hobbyless, insular and have no realistic ambition. But, mostly, the blame must be attached to the lack of amiable communication between people.

The 'give and take' of good conversation must be bolstered up for it is a vital ingredient in public speaking. If you want opponents to listen to you, their viewpoint must also be embodied into your comments. To speak well in public you must actually *like* people, be sincerely interested in their achievements – and tell them so! This goes beyond exchanging drinks over a bar with your own kind. You have to find human beings interesting in all facets and faults, understanding weaknesses without necessarily condoning them. Novelists and biographers possess this intensely valuable attribute, being able to step outside themselves in the study of others rather than the average man who merely assesses the value of everyone he meets in relation to his own career or progress. Those who have nothing material to offer are, of course, intolerantly discarded. So vast numbers of people are knowledge-shy.

Public speaking is a serious responsibility from lighthearted social discourses to rising in parliament. Every function at which you speak will bring its obligations for you to succeed. We cannot change personalities, but we can better ourselves. And you will know that you are popular if people want to talk to you, seek you out, have you in their midst and listen to you because they know that you, too, want to hear from them.

As in public speaking, true conversation is imparting information. Even local gossip is a form of information although perhaps not always passed on for the right reasons – but at least two people are exchanging ideas. Good public speaking is really a solo conversation, but so constructed as to involve question and answer within itself. You have to anticipate queries which may rise in an audience's mind and reply to them yourself so that they do not feel your talk is one-sided or biased. In other words, completely involve them.

Brevity and methods of approach

Be concise. The most voiced criticism of speakers generally is that 'they went on too long'. You must have heard many who committed this common 'sin' in public speaking. Speech-making acts like a drug on some people. They stand up prepared to do ten minutes, but get carried away. They do not think they are boring – but the audience does. Often the cause of over-long speeches is a speaker who clouds his facts with too much personality, is ebullient, winsome, jocular or the stern orator. It is a form of self-glorification and is transparent to most discerning audiences. They see through these ploys and are lynx-eared for the slightest hint of mock-modesty.

So keep it simple but without an over economy of vocabulary so as to make for repetitive phrasing; editing your work to give it interesting form will become a discipline.

Personal satisfaction in public speaking comes from possessing confidence in what you have to say. Take trouble to prepare it and people will listen to you. The abrasive ranters who rise to give vent to disjointed ideas find it hard to get hearings beyond their own minority cliques. They may regard their wild, shapeless ramblings as a form of 'free speech' but forget that there is also the freedom of an audience to choose whether or not they will listen! Certainly they will not strain their intellects to pick out the wheat from the chaff in a dust storm of erratic phrasing. So many speakers with possibly valid arguments fail to make audiences comprehend them through simulating anger in the hope that the cause can be won solely on high decibels.

There are also some speakers whose approach is so inept, so cliché-ridden, that they cannot give *themselves* any satisfaction, let alone an audience. Often such speakers are mature people whose occupations or special positions have, comparatively late in life, suddenly demanded public speaking. Once they could relax in an almost entirely anonymous background; now they have to address board meetings, sit as school governors, talk to young people, their workers on shop floors or address shareholders. Mostly they see this modern need for public utterance as a chore. 'I know my job,' they say to themselves, 'what does it matter how I deliver my information?' So, they expect their ill-prepared speeches to be accepted automatically with a respect they feel due to their exalted position. But, as we know, people are being chosen for posts because they can speak more convincingly in public than their competitors. No one today would appoint an inarticulate shop steward any more than a girls' school's governing body would offer a headship to a nun under a vow of silence! So those who would make progress must take the trouble to speak well both in private and public.

However, we have to be on our guard against expecting instant success. Modern thinking has made it fashionable to exaggerate claims of supremacy. People like to be self-styled 'champions' and there is no honour, as once there was, in being on the losing side.

Unfortunately this restless desire for immediate results without proper training has caused a lowering in standards of public speaking. Lack of rehearsal, dearth of good material or the patience in unearthing it, plus the hit-or-miss tactic of hoping all will be right on the night, will add to a speaker's natural tensions when he or she will finally rise to their feet. Inwardly they are in a blind panic of unpreparedness but outwardly they will endeavour to bluff it out. Soon, lack of experience shows through and their now proven insecurity turns to ugly resentment of the audience. Mostly this is evident on occasions when the speaker has not bothered to gather more than a list of doubtful jokes, entirely unrelated to the theme of the speech. If these fail, he has nothing left.

When you rise to speak you must have in your mind a clearly-defined purpose – that is to inform your audience according to the subject and the purpose of the event. Your material must be appropriate to that theme and your humour, if any, relevant and progressive towards the climax of your speech. If you have taken trouble over these aspects, public speaking nerves will never worry you and you will enjoy to the full the audiences' appreciation of your efforts. It is a pleasant feeling sitting down to sustained applause; that is not vanity, you have a right to feel proud. You have achieved what you set out to do, the audience has listened with enjoyment and they are warmly acknowledging your proficiency. Ezra Pound once said: 'I believe in technique as a test of man's sincerity.' You are certainly being insincere with audiences if you do not acquire the skill to do the job properly.

Speak well in public and you can be invaluable to your community, for it may well mean that you may have to speak up for those unable to speak for themselves. But, above all, you will have the satisfaction of being able to speak up for *yourself*.

2

Making the Best of your Voice

Your vocal chords are instruments of communication. Your brain provides the score from which they will play. In public speaking, even before worrying about what you are going to say, the care of your voice and how you use it is of paramount importance.

Only you will know the timbre and pitch of your personal voice box. But, be it high, low or middle register, you are stuck with it. Do *not* on any account try and alter it. Perhaps it seems strange to stress this but many new speakers, dissatisfied with their true pitch, strive hard to change it, usually affecting deeper than normal tones. It is understandable in the search for perfection – but highly dangerous. Sustaining a false range will create further strain beyond the other tensions of addressing audiences. Raising or lowering your natural tone comes automatically within your ordinary compass but to stretch the vocal chords beyond their designed limit is not only injurious but is extremely difficult, if not impossible, to sustain throughout a speech. Many servicemen and women who remember their first drill command on a barrack square will understand this point. When they had not yet mastered projection they ended that parade either hoarse or completely speechless. So, too, will speakers who stretch their vocal chords beyond the limit nature has ordained for them.

Often falsifying the voice comes from a subconscious desire to 'act' a speech, a fault common to some beginners. They rise to their feet to give a 'performance' outside their natural selves. They are being, of course unwittingly, insincere to their audience, confusing a stage role with a public speaking engagement. It is up to you to mould your real vocal chords into a viable sound box for what you have to say, completely within normal range.

Projecting your voice, especially when using a microphone, is simple if you have no extra worries about vocal acrobatics. Often a criticism of a speaker made by friends is that he or she did not sound a bit like their normal self! This leads to ridicule especially if cracks are heard when concentration lapses which cause a wavering of timbre. Add to that 'imitation voice' a flowery unnatural vocabulary completely unlike the speaker's ordinary dialogue, and a poor 'character' performance is the result.

Once you are aware of your voice and its limitations you will speak well within that compass. If you hear your voice on tape it can at first perhaps be an unnerving experience! None of us in everyday life ever hears our voices as they really are owing to the bone structure of our ears. When on tape most people are horrified because they inevitably think they speak more deeply than they actually do. So, in a moment of panic, they try to sink their voice. Your speaking responsibilities are great enough without this added burden.

Few of us possess downright jarring voices and, even if you sound harsher than you would wish, you can by compromise on pitch, still obtain a good balance of projection. Many gravel-voiced speakers use a quiet approach avoiding really high registers so that they are always in control. Your voice is part of your personality and often the adjustment is merely a matter of speaking a little more slowly than in normal conversation.

But whatever your personal sound no audience will complain if your words are uttered clearly and your subject is covered with apposite vocabulary.

Dialects

Most of us possess a form of inherited pronunciation, for our background has dictated our voices. To some it is an asset; to others from more remote regions it might be considered a handicap. But never lose your own dialect. Attempts to eradicate regional brogues in Britain, for example, in favour of the so-called Oxford accent led many speakers in early generations to affect an ultra-correct phrasing and use a 'foreign' vocabulary. In consequence they became figures of fun on public platforms – members of parliament, town mayors and toastmasters among them. A personal dialect is a legacy to be treasured. But it must also be considered very carefully when you are addressing audiences far from your birthplace.

As Britons in other English-speaking countries have found with their various dialects, 'Geordie', 'Brummagen', 'Cockney', 'Scouse' or variations of Scottish, Welsh and Irish local 'brogues', their speeches have sometimes been hard to get across because of their various idiosyncrasies. Texans and those born in the Bronx have faced similar problems when in different States or overseas. One prime example is the intrusive 'r' which in the south of England makes the word 'pass' or 'chance' into 'parss' and 'charnce'. The midlands and north of Britain never insert that 'r'. Such variations in pronunciation are manifold the world over. Different locations use different frameworks for the same word. An Englishman will say 'in a little while' whereas the true Scot will use the much more alliterative 'in a wee while'.

Thus you have to ensure that both your pronunciation and vocabulary is crystal clear so that your 'foreign' presentation does not mystify your audience. When preparing a speech or lecture you must take into account exactly where you are speaking and to whom. To parody the old adage, when in Rome you will want the Romans to understand you. It may well mean speaking at a slower tempo, even elaborating points in more detail than you would on more familiar home ground. To achieve this you must analyse your own dialect thoroughly for an audience not to understand you is a confession of personal failure. It would be arrogance to insist that your listeners must accept your dialect and its peculiarities when they were born a thousand miles away from your district. So you give yourself every chance of success by considering them to the utmost.

But do not try to alter your natural dialect physically. It is precious and must not die out. You can avoid 'local' colloquialisms, or, if you must use them, also explain them. Overseas audiences love such snippets of information. For example in Yorkshire they often say 'brass' for 'money', a well-used slang term. So you tell that to an uninitiated audience and you will also entertain as well as instruct. There are thousands of examples, New Yorkers say 'sidewalk', Londoners say 'pavement', then there is 'elevator' and 'lift' ... and so on. In all it is a vastly interesting study and can only be fully understood by inter-communication of dialogue throughout the world.

One of the fascinations of English-speaking dialects is that they have become fused into its teaching. Colloquialisms and grammatical construction detected in foreign students' speech sometimes enable us to tell exactly from which district, state or county their instructor came, either in Britain, Australia, Canada, West Indies or the USA. This is all to the good because dialects add enormously to the character of public speaking.

Over recent years there has been a cult among student-age bodies to cultivate what they term a 'classless' speech, designed, it would seem, to defeat what they feel is a dialogue élitism. But the result is very limiting, a flat monotone, much repetition of the same phrase, devoid of imaginative vocabulary and dull in the extreme which is quite inadequate for the public platform. If you wish to persuade or commentate on a subject, you must also sound interesting, colourful and entertaining.

Good speech is not 'class' or mere affectation in a strataed society, it is commonsense to speak clearly so that fullest communication is achieved in an interesting manner.

The telephone test

Anyone who uses a phone well usually has the makings of a good public speaker. In fact one ruse employed by function organisers and speaking agents who have been recommended an unknown speaker is to telephone him or her. Thus by a protracted call they can assess their possibilities. It is an almost infallible test. Anyone who can, over the wire, evince the interest of a complete stranger – and especially make them laugh – is a promising public speaker. Provided all other aspects of the right metabolism and stamina are there, the engaging telephone personality should do well in front of audiences.

Yet, despite the invention of the telephone well over a hundred years ago, some managements today still despair of finding good, reliable telephone operators. In fact the standard has declined since the 1950s and there are some who man switchboards who remain nothing more than a minimal answering service. If your opposite number is not available to take your call, an inanimate voice will express no willingness to help further, often parroting a set procedure beyond which they will not go. They are transparently obvious to hurry you off the line and not bother them further. They are both unhelpful to you and the firm which employs them.

The problem again is lack of vocabulary. They are basically afraid of the telephone because it is constantly bringing them into contact with fluent people. Every time a call comes in a more eloquent person makes that operator more deeply aware of his or her own limitations in dialogue. So they clam up, take only routine steps but never initiative. This is another terrible example that, with man on the moon, natural, easy and interesting conversation is receding between ordinary people.

With business pressures mounting daily, competition turning from keen to cut-throat in world markets, telephones must be manned by astute, quick-thinking young persons with good vocabularies and a balanced sense of speech. It is, in itself, a form of public speaking, putting strangers at ease and sounding personally involved in a desire to help if the proper recipient of the call is not available.

Good 'phone voices are rare gems among young staff. So if you possess clear diction, either on the switchboard or at the reception desk, start thinking more ambitiously about using it in different speaking roles within the firm. Employers, too, should be looking within their own ranks for fluent speakers who can read minutes and handle seminar work.

People with fine speaking voices do not always know how to make the best of them – or indeed that they possess such a valuable attribute at all. Only those who hear them can be certain of it, so it is up to them to bring them forward.

Care of the voice

Health plays a vital part in public speaking. Feeling below par adds to nerves when facing audiences. You must keep fit to behave naturally on a public platform. Sometimes you will have to try and galvanise into action when feeling low and sluggish but that is understandable and only a temporary set-back. However if your general health is below standard, you are over-weight or take little exercise, you will create unnecessary strain on yourself.

If you do not smoke so much the better. But if you do, use your public speaking training to cut it down. Smoking is not good for speakers. However, many public speakers find smoking a solace and use it to soothe the nerves.

As prevention is better than cure, gentle gargling with half a teaspoon of salt in a tumbler of water, well stirred, is one of the oldest yet still one of the best remedies.

Alcohol is the biggest menace in the speaking world. It is not good for the throat, but often has to be consumed before speaking in the comparatively harmless ritual of toasts. Gentle wines will not affect the vocal chords but spirits unless well watered can. In moderation alcohol is so often an intrinsic part of public speaking functions. It only becomes an enemy when over-used as Dutch courage.

But if your throat is sore or dry after a speaking stint, honey stirred into warm milk is a wonderful palliative. One speaker in our acquaintance used to take a spoonful of Vaseline before speaking – but this inevitably upset his near neighbours at dining tables!

Speaking after big meals is an obstacle we all have to overcome. At luncheons and dinners the luckiest public speakers are those who are not gourmands. A conscientious public speaker will treat such official meals as a weight-watcher might and eat sparingly of each course so that, when his turn comes to speak, he does not feel bloated and distended. If, as can happen in the first days of public speaking, you find you have rushed your meal – a sign that you are subconsciously trying to hurry forward that moment of truth when you get to your feet –

you will find indigestion a great hazard to concentration when you are finally announced. The decision must be yours but you will be better off eating lightly if your speech is of importance. It may be a compliment to the chef to belch – but not during a speech, in front of an audience!

Breathing

Proper breath control, inhaling through the nose and exhaling from the mouth, is essential for easy public speaking. Nerves caused by the significance of the occasion can tighten chest muscles and constrict the diaphragm. Thus, if you are already a shallow breather you can, through tension, breathe even more restrictedly so that, when you face your audience, you appear to be panting. As initial nerves can make a new speaker inclined to race, to gabble his words, if this is combined by shortage of breath and bad control, clarity is completely defeated.

Deep breathing in pure open air is the best exercise for the public speaker. Any chest expanding exercise is valuable, throwing arms wide and retracting them when breathing evenly. Arm rotating is also useful – in fact any athlete's chest exercises are essential especially those which give the lungs a chance to expand and function fully.

A good walk, not necessarily striding out but at a firm, normal pace, works wonders especially if you find a path by the sea. But for good breathing exercise it is better to keep on a level surface rather than clamber over rocks which is liable to take the mind off the full concentration of inhaling and exhaling. The cult of 'jogging' is good in very short spells, but do not end up physically tired. Contain your exercises so that fatigue does not undo all your efforts. To speak well the blood must be flowing normally, the head kept clear and the body relaxed. As has been mentioned before there is bound to be mental strain in the early days of public speaking; that is why the body should be in a peak condition. If you are also off-colour your mental anxieties are doubled to make your speech an ordeal which might be obvious to the audience. So, keep fit – and more than halve your initial worries.

Speaking and driving

Following a long journey hunched at the wheel many professional speakers take a brief but brisk stroll after parking the car. This is good thinking. A throbbing, frustrating trip down motorways can fatigue you much more than you realise at the time. And if you have witnessed a nasty pile-up, or suffered inefficient driving by others you will need that walk to unwind.

While invaluable to all generations, this exercise is particularly valid for the more mature speakers who, however experienced on the platform, are more vulnerable to fatigue. Youngsters, too, should get into this loosening-up habit before facing audiences. Just a short stroll lasting about seven minutes at a sharp pace is all that is required, and will do the trick to tone up muscles and clear the mind.

After a speaking engagement it is again advisable to relax before setting out on the return journey. Leaping straight into the driving seat with the applause still ringing in your ears is very bad for concentration at the wheel. You will, especially in the early days of public speaking, be inclined to mull over the relative success of your speech while tackling the traffic on perhaps strange roads. An unwinding period before you leave is advised if it is possible, clearing your mind of any speech 'post-mortem' – or there might be a real one!

If it is an evening engagement, it is better to stay the night and not drive again until you are fresh and fit next morning. Usually, at evening functions, there is plenty of liquid hospitality from your hosts, so a hotel bed is better than the risk of an accident through sleepiness and drink.

Generally driving and public speaking do not mix well. So ensure you have extra time both on arrival and when you depart so that you do not carry the tension from one activity to the other.

Voice strain

The microphone, the technique of which we discuss later, is more or less in constant use today so that it is rare that you will have to strain your vocal chords beyond lifting your pitch slightly above conversational level.

But there remain those vibrant, rhetorical 'performers' who strain their neck muscles, turn puce-cheeked and quiver to demonstrate their intensity of purpose. All quite unnecessary. Audiences are more likely to be embarrassed than impressed by over-dramatic presentations. The quiet or moderate speakers who make points clearly without attempting to break the sound barrier are always more successful.

In any case getting yourself worked up into a frenzy is not good public speaking despite the fact that some politicians seem to think the public gullible enough to mistake sound volume for sincerity. Emphasis is not best achieved by adding crescendos. Public speakers, genuinely feeling anger, control themselves. They will smoulder rather than rant, using longer pauses to maintain discipline over themselves. But they certainly do not risk damage to their vocal chords. The motto is – be mellow, don't bellow.

Using the mouth correctly

A fault in early public speaking can be lack of full use of the available jaw movement. Projection and enunciation of words are lost through speaking with lips insufficiently opened. You see it in schools when children, not trained to speak with clarity at home, talk through clenched teeth rather than give their jaws proper expansion. Others speak from the side of the mouth as if imparting an old-tyme stage aside. Both are sometimes inaudible to the sharpest ear. The impression left by speakers bedevilled by either of these disabilities is that of a vast inferiority complex, as if half-ashamed of everything they mumble.

Naturally one must also avoid the other extreme in speaking, the lips oval-shaped, every syllable seeming to be masticated as Victorian elocution teachers once mouthed 'prunes' and 'prisms' to make children recite far too precisely for naturalness at family parties.

As a guide the mouth should be opened more in a public

speech than in normal face-to-face conversation but only at three-quarter width, never the full dark cavern which a dentist might require for an inspection. We leave that stretch for singers. Self-consciousness or over-conscientiousness in your desire to allow your hearers a clear diction often brings about the exaggerated mouth shape. Lips at full stretch leave no room for a snap correction to any slip of the tongue without it being completely obvious. Once your face becomes in any way contorted it will distract the audience concentration upon your words which, as we know, is the whole point of public speaking.

Training yourself for a good delivery

Reading aloud is excellent preparation for speech-making. Any undertaking from telling the children stories at bedtime to reading minutes at meetings, will increase your experience in fluency. A chapter or two from a novel or instructional manual not only allows you to 'hear' your delivery but also adds to your vocabulary so keep a dictionary by you when an unfamiliar word crops up. This continual practice of feeling words flow from your mouth as your brain releases them allows you increased familiarity with phrasing.

A role or two in local dramatic productions is a great asset as those will, in addition to increasing your word power and projection, give you a true 'feel' of audience reaction. Play reading societies are also a great boon for, again, you will come across new words, new phrases (possibly you will also find some useful quotations for future speeches) and also allow you to study change of mood for anecdotal characterisation.

Seize every opportunity you can to exercise your vocabulary, speak at meetings and debates, read the lesson in church, converse more freely with both friend and stranger. Get used, all you can, to finding yourself, even for a moment or two, in the spotlight so that facing audiences in the future becomes easy and comfortable. You will find in life that so many opportunities arise in which you can take the initiative if you are already equipped to do so. Often from lack of confidence in making a split second decision, a chance is lost forever. Being able to speak in public is the greatest asset you can possess in coping with unexpected situations. The ability sharpens your reactions; you can take charge if necessary.

Above all listen to more experienced speakers. Don't copy them in style, be yourself at all costs, but absorb their experience and their repose. And always keep within the range of your personal sound box.

3

Speech Presentation

Few untrained speakers are ever mindful of speech presentation, that is, the harmonious blending of subject and delivery. 'Presentation', in other words, means giving your text exactly the right treatment, both in timing and demeanour. As you will see in the next chapter on drafting speeches, the subject must be pertinent to the occasion and obviously you would not prepare an entirely irrelevant script. But even the most appropriate wording can, through nervousness in first-time speeches, be delivered in entirely the wrong manner. Being off-key like this is understandable when tensed up by the occasion and the strain of remembering your lines but, now forewarned, we can obviate this fault here and now.

Mood and manner must fuse smoothly. You must give your words their true character, minus twitching frowns, for example, when you tell an audience you are enjoying yourself! Top-class speakers present their speeches with voice and brain in complete harmony, the tone matching the text. While this concord may seem obvious, it is as not as common as one thinks. Speeches can be made as if Hamlet's lines are being spoken by Bottom the Weaver. The fault lies in the speakers saying their speeches as a role learned by heart rather than it actually coming from the heart. Their tone is drab when it should be lively, they sound facetious when they should be witty, they sound irate when indulging in a very mild rebuke. They are not being wittingly insincere; it is just that their anxiety shows through and they pump the words out with the wrong light and shade.

Vocal hesitances

Rarely is even a good speech entirely devoid of the 'ums' and 'ers' of everyday indecision. These 'hiccups of speech' are caused when the brain and vocal chords suddenly 'slip a cog' and become temporarily out of tune with each other. For a few seconds they misfire, the brain failing to register sense to the tongue and smooth synchronisation is momentarily lost. Often a public speaker is not personally to blame when this happens during a speech. An interruption from the audience, a cough or sneeze, or, at a dinner, a sudden crash of crockery from the adjacent kitchen ... low flying aircraft during a conference ... or a police siren beyond the council chambers ... there are hundreds of these 'surprise' hazards which can throw a speaker into these hesitances when the train of thought has been rudely interrupted. Thus the brain abruptly cuts off the supply of intelligent material to the voice.

When such breaks in concentration occur a speaker instinctively feels he or she must fill the gap and plough on with some sort of sound, however meaningless, to show the audience the voice is still functioning during the lapse. It is a worldwide abstraction – but still remains always a distraction. Some speakers only use 'er' occasionally, it being inbred into their normal conversation, but others find these useless noises increase when standing before an audience. They imply that the speaker is trying to assure his hearers that there is more to come but he has not yet got to grips with the sense of it!

If instead of these 'ums', 'ahs' and 'ers', however, we could substitute a *pause*, to give the brain time to get into matching stride with the voice again, fluency of delivery is maintained. Silence is more effective than filling it meaninglessly. Try, if you can, to train yourself to use a pause in such circumstances so that you gather your wits in silence. If there is no outside interference but you are actually stuck for a word, you are more likely to recall it during a quiet moment than further obstructing your own line of thought by uttering gibberish.

Of course one cannot be expected to lose these conversational hesitances right away; indeed, as we have stressed, some speakers suffer these miniscule falterings for life. They would not appear in a written transcript of the speech afterwards but, if recorded on tape, every vocal blemish remains to embarrass them. Most of us will never quite reach perfection of absolute unbroken continuity every time we rise to speak but we can still attain a degree of sharp thinking. If you remember in our early training that a pause is more effective than stalling for time with vocal gobbledigook, the better will be your speech presentation.

Appearance when speaking

Watch yourself in a mirror when you are rehearsing a speech. Not with the notes in your hand but when you have more or less committed to memory what you wish to say. Are you a gulping-type appearing to swallow hard after every sentence? Do you, henlike, peck forward as you utter? Are you, when imparting what you feel to be a particularly apt phrase, liable to emphasise it by tilting your head sideways? If so this can make you appear unwittingly winsome, coy or arch! Do your hands thresh the air as you try and engender extra impact? Do you shrug or hunch your shoulders continually? Do your hands get in the way when you are on your feet?

We see such sufferers being interviewed on television. They wriggle, rock their heads, clench and unclench hands, clasp knees, straighten ties, pat hair or fiddle with medallions. Perhaps, if they are already famous in other fields, their mannerisms can be forgiven. Being familiar figures already, exaggerated gestures will not distract the audience from what they are saying. But for a non-celebrity, any restless movement is a great handicap. Being strangers to the audience they will be 'viewed' by first appearance values so that the essence of what they have to say is lost if magnified gestures attract the eyes of the listeners and not their ears. After all the reason you are being interviewed is for what you have to *say*!

Good speakers remain as still as possible. They use movement so sparingly that when they do make a gesture it really does usefully emphasise a particular point. Certainly they turn their heads evenly to encompass the audience to left and right of the microphone, but it is never a jerked, intense movement. Nor do they fix their eyes on the wall opposite and remain like stone statues looking ahead all the time. They may well use their eyes cleverly to underline phrases, raising or lowering them as the situation under discussion warrants, even to narrowing them for simulated self bewilderment or widening them for mock surprise.

Mostly, of course, such eye movements are best used in anecdotal contexts. If you are recounting a dialogue between two or more characters in your illustration, the eyes help the narration considerably. A speaker may not go completely into 'acting' the characters in an anecdote but he or she can make token gestures both facially and vocally using the eyes to denote reaction and, if skilful enough, switch into an apposite dialect. Thus an anecdote can be made to sound extremely authentic and give a speech atmosphere and contrast.

However, there are still a host of irritating habits which mar good speaking. Fidgeting with spectacles for example, a speaker may need them to read notes, but continually takes them off to face the audience, jabbing them back crookedly when he needs his mind refreshed. This is time consuming and loses fluency, the gaps being filled usually with 'ums' and 'ahs' as the head lowers again to find the lost place in the notes. Either wear your glasses all the time or dispense with them altogether. If your notes are made in bold lettering you may well be able to avoid the constant 'seesaw' of glasses.

When you rise to speak a relaxed stance is important. This can be achieved by placing the legs slightly apart and putting the weight on the balls of the feet so that you tilt forward very slightly. Sink back on the heels and your calf muscles will tire if you stand for a longish period. Leaning back also makes you liable to jerk your head forward instinctively trying to compensate for loss of distance between you and the microphone and present a jutting jaw effect.

For men stance is comparatively simple but for ladies in high heels adjustment has to be made so as not to appear to be leaning in towards the audience. Many experienced lady speakers at dinners kick off their shoes under the table when they stand to speak so that they can get the same balance as a man in flatter footwear.

Do not hold or 'fondle' the microphone stand. It is a temptation to grip on to something in early speaking but the microphone should be untouched by hand! You can accidentally rock it out of alignment and cause distortions. Hold your notes just below the chest and so avoid them rustling which can sound like an express train leaving a tunnel on a delicate microphone. Do not speak too close to it. Beginners often feel obliged to almost kiss it in an effort to be heard. Usually three to four inches away is sufficient but the higher the standard of microphone, the more latitude you have. Even then, if it is a single stem, you have to ensure it is far enough away to pick up your voice when you turn your head slightly. If you are too close, the slightest deviation left or right will make you suddenly inaudible. But when you are a celebrity you may well stand up to a row of strategically placed microphones, like tulips all round to encompass every section you may wish to address at given points of your speech.

Hands often do present a problem in early speaking. Once you allow yourself to be conscious of them, you are apt to indulge in all sorts of gymnastics to get rid of them. Lapels are gripped, arms are folded – a very uncomfortable stance indeed – chins are stroked, elbows are cupped, hands rest unnaturally on hips. The worst pose a man can effect is put his hands in pockets. He may think it looks casual or relaxed, but it can give a rather patronising air as if the speaker is just obliging the audience in passing, which can offend more critical members. Ladies sometimes twist and twirl necklaces. New speakers, trying to assume a nonchalance they do not inwardly feel, change positions far too often which is distracting. Your stance, once comfortable, should remain constant – and still.

Holding your notes can help. But if these can be left on the table below or you are speaking without them, allow the arms to hang loosely at your sides. Hands are most easily forgotten in that position! However you can join them, knuckle under palm in front of you or ladies can clasp hands, interlocking the fingers – but the arms themselves should always remain loose and easy. Men can put hands behind the back but, we repeat, the best attitude is dropping arms limply from the shoulders down beside you. Once you start connecting your hands together you become automatically conscious of them and what may start as a relaxed attitude can become fidgety if hands are in any way gripped together.

Beware of over-using hand movement. A quick hand spread (not a wide circling movement), a pointed finger or short shoulder shrug often serve to underline points, but these will come naturally as they do in conversation. If simulated they are apt to be exaggerated contortions.

A good speaker will never use the same gesture twice in one speech. That is excellent stagecraft as is the use of pauses to gain effect. If, for example, a particularly subtle reference is made, a long pause allows it to dawn on and penetrate the audience's minds – and, if humorous, the laughter may begin as a ripple and then break into a roar as the full impact hits them. But rush on without that pause and the point is lost forever. So pause and give your audience time to digest the more intricate parts of your discourse.

In presenting a speech, however nervous you may feel, you must rehearse yourself to appear sufficiently in charge for the audience to have confidence in you. So keep as still as possible and do not be lured into the mistaken theory that every new aspect of your speech needs a change of pose.

Integrity

Your approach must be faithful to your subject. If you have to propose a toast to an individual which involves your praising him, you should never use that sort of speech as a vehicle to implant your own personality upon the audience. Once you forget the sincerity of the occasion and try and indulge in a little one-upmanship you are failing in your brief. Some speakers seem unable to resist self-aggrandisement in any speech they make.

Above all you must avoid 'meiosis' – a common trait among

speakers desirous of personally impressing an audience. Meiosis is a species of hyperbole representing a thing to be less than it is. In public speaking it takes the form of blowing up a comparatively unimportant event to cover the mention of a much more significant one which is not relevant to the subject. As for example if your topic is traffic problems, a speaker out to impress might say: 'I'd just left The White House after seeing the President when I witnessed this dreadful accident. Two cars skidded....' The motoring aspect is valid to his theme – but he has not been able to resist slipping in that other self-important detail for his own glorification. But audiences are shrewd and the sort of egotism displayed by meiosis only estranges them from this type of speaker. In fact any speaker appearing to grant himself a form of élitism over his audiences is headed for some very tepid receptions.

Speakers bring disappointments on themselves more by overdoing the personality ploy than through being nervous. Trying hard to be 'popular', they use their subject as a prop for their own image rather than for its true value. Perhaps such speakers are influenced by television stars who contrive to appear good-natured, easy goin', so-likable people even to wishing God to bless us when they finish their act. This of course is just show-business razamatazz. These apparently amiable gestures, these words of comfort such as asking the audience 'to be kind to each other' cover 'charismas' which are all part of the big-sell of hard-headed commerce. The motives are entirely different from any public speaking engagement but newcomers to it are apt to try and embody showbiz ballyhoo into the speech world.

Stagey technique on the speaking platform will not turn you into an instant, 'super' personality. Once you start employing artificial methods to enhance it, you will lose it altogether. You are not in public speaking to give a performance of yourself but to appear always completely in your own true colours. As you should not change your natural voice, so you cannot alter your inborn personality.

Sometimes it is apparent when a woman tries to show she, too, can be racey, tough and uncompromising. But such a presentation can well prove a failure because that approach is off-key with the audience. She is 'acting' the speech and they know it, having realised very early on that she is not presenting a true picture of herself. Women have to be far more subtle than that. The best female politicians never forget they are women when delivering hard-hitting diatribes. But there have been others in office who tried to act the Amazon with sometimes sad results – especially at election times.

Your job is to please your audiences wherever you are: they are the judges of your success, not you. You may find you have to alter pre-conceived notions about your speeches when some aspects fail at first, but if you are true to your subject, the audience will be true to you.

A veteran speaker once said: 'Audiences often forget the name of a good speaker as they have been too absorbed in his words to read it on the menu ... but a *bad* speaker's name is always remembered....'

Pace, rhythm and timing

Because of nerves learners are apt to race their initial speeches. It is a natural instinct to get on with the job – but that over-eagerness so often leads to loss of clarity through gabbling. Alternatively a slow delivery at funereal pace not only bores people but allows them to be a jump ahead of anything such a speaker says. So remember that guideline again, speak only slightly slower than in normal conversation and give the words a shade more projection and volume.

Pace is vitally important in public speaking. The right, even pace will come with practice as an actor learns a part and delivers it on stage with correct emphasis and pauses to give his lines the best possible effect. So study your own speaking style closely. If you are apt to drawl, you will have to develop more attack in your speaking, be crisper. If you are inclined to race with words falling over each other, take more breaths between sentences, cultivate the pause and generally keep yourself in check.

You will have to be quite candid with yourself over these traits. If you have friends or family who will give you a guaranteed sincere appraisal of your voice and its natural pace, seek their help in adjustment. Do not regard it as weakness to ask such a favour. Their criticism may be just what you need and determine your success and failure.

Hearing yourself on tape is also extremely useful. The fact that you are recording may well bring improvement immediately from the too-hurried or too-laboured delivery simply because you are entirely conscious of your objective. But it is no good fooling yourself. However good your material, it will not stand up by itself if you lack correct light and shade, pace and rhythm. Important points can be emphasised by a slowing of tempo, the lighter moments quickened, especially when building up to a climax. A change of subject always needs a slower approach so that your audience has time to adjust to the new train of thought and will not confuse it with the last.

We discuss preparation of material later but it is important to realise how pauses, changes of tempo and heavy or light emphasis can affect the construction of your speech. Each section needs a balanced rhythm so that the material is heard from your lips to best advantage. A serious aspect in your speech may need the voice lowered slightly whereas a humorous anecdote can require perhaps a sharper, higher pitch, possibly indicating your own 'surprise' at the dénouement to underline the fun.

'Timing' is not the specified length of your speech as set by the organisers (although this, too, is important) but the actual 'timing' of your spoken words. It can best be illustrated by the good joke teller and the bad. The former gives you the facts concisely, builds up to the climax with effective pauses and emphasis, never uses irrelevancies or gets side-tracked, and gives full impact to the ultimate laugh line. The latter, however, will ruin it by not being sure of certain points ('It was not a Tuesday, it was a Wednesday'), omit vital information ('Oh, I forgot to tell you the man was a plumber') and he can even foul up the story right at the opening by saying 'Have you heard the one about the man who . . .' and then reveal the tag line upon which the final laugh depends!

Timing is constructing the information of a speech correctly, giving each aspect of your topic's development perfect balance and emphasis in relation to the context and completing it on exactly the proper note. Every professional speaker – like an actor – needs good timing. Some are born with it, others have to acquire it through diligence – which means rehearsal. If an actor does not 'time' his lines correctly the replies he receives from fellow players will sound lame and off-key.

The timing of pauses, too, is vital. Pauses allow points to sink in so that the audience retains sufficient information to link with the climax of each phase when it arrives.

Watch a good stand-up comedian as he handles a 'live' audience. Notice how he pauses to avoid talking into laughs – or, if he does, immediately retracts and repeats the line that might have been missed in an unexpected guffaw. Then, when he is sure the audience have got the point, he moves on to his punch line. That 'timing' discipline is needed in public speaking even if the entertaining style is different. If humour is to play an important part in your public speaking, good 'timing' is essential.

It is also of paramount importance if you have a dull subject to handle. You have to ensure that your listeners understand every aspect without being bored. Rush the data because it also bores you and the whole exercise becomes a waste of time. School teachers and instructors should all possess precise timing if they are to be effective in their jobs.

Timing is setting a correct pace, knowing where to speed up and slow down, where to pause, where to insert the information, getting the material in the right order and delivering it as flawlessly as possible. An early fault is constantly dropping the voice down at the end of sentences. Another is starting in a higher pitch than necessary and then tailing off. It is also the art of making a question mark actually 'sound' in your delivery when ending a sentence, not with a low finality but with the voice raised to indicate the need for an answer to follow.

Study of television and radio news readers is a very good exercise in the study of timing. They know just where emphasis and underlining is needed, where to insert pauses in their scripts, both long and short. Their experience tells them exactly how to balance each sentence according to its overall value to the item. And, without panic, they can blandly apologise for a slip of the tongue and proceed unruffled to show how completely in control they are. But if you are considered a good conversationalist and people find you interesting then you must already possess an instinctive sense of timing.

As you gain experience you will probably make the same speech many times – most of us have a regular standby – which, because you know every nuance of it through repetition, will become perfectly timed by you. To that add the confidence that association with audiences has also brought you and then public speaking will become a true pleasure. Gone then will be the days when it was a rather chancy experience in which you hoped for the best – but expected the worst!

Feeling off form

It is noticeable, sometimes, that a practised speaker is not entirely in harmony with the audience at the onset. They have not laughed at his first anecdote and a weary look crosses his face. The mask has slipped, but only momentarily. He steels himself and presses on. In such circumstances he may well simulate a bonhomie he does not feel, but he is at least being fair on his audience. While the organisers may be guilty of poor arrangements or he has had a bad day at the office, which are perhaps reasons enough for that lack of rapport, it is certainly not the fault of the audience. So with all the sincerity he can muster that speaker lifts himself out of personal doldrums and gets cracking to amuse or instruct them. School teachers with splitting headaches who have to cope with wayward or lively children have the same problem – but they have to stick at it too.

When you are experienced and your material and timing is strong, being slightly less than a hundred per cent fit will not pose traumatic problems. If you have a cold, tell the audience. Do not over-excuse yourself but take them into your confidence. Indeed if the audience is really receptive it can effect a better cure than a doctor's prescription!

Drink and drugs

Speakers who rely on a couple of gins or a pep pill or two, even if they may get away with it a few times, are inevitably caught out. However liberal your hosts or your confidence in your own capacity, never use liquor as a regular stimulus before you speak in public. Once your system gets used to artificial boosting it will always need it and there will come the time when it is not available. Nothing is more pathetic than the ageing speaker gazing wildly round when he realises the bar is not open at a morning event in the town hall. Mostly he will resort to a hip flask to get himself going.

Only you can judge your own capacity for liquor and those who boast a large intake eventually make fools of themselves as they grow older. The spectacle of either an inebriated or drugged speaker or, tragically, one suffering from the effects of mixing the two – is not as rare as it should be. To some alcohol or pills are as necessary as bread and water is to normal diet. Drugs and drink can exaggerate or considerably restrict the normal body functions. Both distort perception and normal behaviour. Obviously there must be a limit to stretching nature's limits artificially. So, the afflicted speaker, when on his feet, begins to wander from the point, diction becomes slurred and absurdities and spoonerisms set in. The audience becomes more and more embarrassed as the swaying, befuddled speaker tries to giggle his way out of trouble. Then, perhaps, a sharp request to sit down – and the speaker loses his temper. This is an appalling situation for both audience and organisers – and in the morning only the speaker himself cannot remember what happened. But everyone else has a ghastly indelible memory of the fiasco.

Mostly these show-downs happen on more informal occasions. It also happens at firms' functions when the staff let their hair – and themselves – down in front of their colleagues. A drunk or drug affected speech can ruin the whole evening. Other speakers having to follow such a spectacle have little chance of getting the audience back to normality, and feel insulted, especially if they are giving their services free. If the audience too, have had to pay for tickets into the bargain, the organisers have a lot of explaining to do.

So do use alcohol warily. At a luncheon, or after-dinner speech, one can easily judge the amount of drink you can allow yourself without presenting your speech out of harmony. But do not become reliant upon it. The extra glass may make you feel on top of the world when you rise but, with the normal speaking tensions, you may find your speech suddenly becoming impaired, your mind reacting sluggishly to the lines you have prepared. Even those who feel their wits are sharpened by drink often find themselves in trouble with unintended insults which have flown from their mouth as they see the world in a magnified, rosy but out of focus, haze. What they think then is a funny ad lib might be in the worst of taste. And if the occasion happens to be bound up with their jobs the consequences can be dire.

As for drugs, if for real health reasons you are obliged to take them, consult your doctor first. Ask him how they will affect your public speaking, how many pills you should take before an engagement, if they will mix with alcohol and what side effects there could be. Quite splendid speakers have cracked up in this way. Having been put on a course of drugs they forget and drink wine or spirits – and after they have been on their feet rambling for a few moments their hitherto unblemished record is in tatters.

There is no artificial stimulus for public speaking. You have to face audiences as yourself, present your true face and make the best of it. And, as confidence grows, that best becomes automatically higher and higher in standard. But it will sink into the depths if there is disharmony between mind and enunciation.

In speaking circuits the word soon gets round. A speaker with a drink problem, however much he may disguise it when on his feet, can also be an awfully expensive liability in the bar afterwards. Club officials soon put his weakness on the grapevine to avoid other organisers suffering in like manner.

So do not drink and talk drivel. Always remember your responsibility both to your audience and your own image.

4

Gathering Material for Speeches

Making sure of your facts

Wherever you are speaking in public you, of course, arm your-self with the full facts of your brief. Most speeches have a set subject, be it part of your job or within your social round when you might be selected to propose or reply to a toast at a civic function. But the same also applies to speaking in committee or at business conferences. Your facts must be right, be they trading figures or progress reports on projects or individuals. You have to be ready with true coverage. The audience listen-ing to you expect nothing but cast-iron exactitude.

In public speaking facts are paramount. We occasionally read of newspaper or television reporters ending up in court facing libel or slander charges as a result of publishing hearsay evidence made upon personal judgments which later proved unfounded. Heavy damages result. But the fine is not as damaging as the reporter's loss of integrity. Sometimes, to be fair to him, we can read between the lines and see that his reported interpreta-tion of the plaintiff's motives was probably true but no hypocrisy of intent could actually be proved. Thus, if they do not come to light as irrevocable facts, then those who contrive to justify them are in trouble.

If you cannot check or substantiate a fact, leave it out. Often a speaker will risk quoting a well-known public figure – only to hear from the body of the hall – 'it wasn't Churchill who said that, it was Eisenhower....' So that speaker loses face and becomes fallible for the rest of the speech. He has taken a chance, not done his homework – and so through laziness, loses out. Once one of your facts is proved wrong, your listeners will doubt the veracity of the rest of your statements. 'Duplicity' is a hard tag to live down.

As facts are the main ingredient of all speeches, you must check and double check them. However you illustrate them, by anecdote, quotation or even by inserting some obvious elaborating fiction, allowable in certain more light-hearted talks, the basic fact upon which you rely must be concrete truth.

Use your local library, ring up experts or write to them so that you have an answer on paper ... take every step you can to verify each item. We all know the political ploys of distorting or twisting facts to suit particular ideologies as seen at public meetings and on the television screen. Interpretations are put upon solid facts which may be far from the original premise but, again, you have to be certain of the basic fact foundation before refuting what you may feel is a spurious conception of it. Being well-briefed in facts will always make you a good political speaker in the gamesmanship of proving opponents wrong. But if *you* are proved wrong when challenged, your reliability as a public speaker will be severely damaged. Even when, later, you may have a sound case to expound upon, there will always be those who will trot out your previous gaffe and use it against you on new issues.

We have stressed sincerity already – and that of course includes being sure of your facts.

Filing systems

Most conscientious speakers keep reference files. They extract newspaper cuttings, keep a notebook handy by the television set or radio, or in a handbag or pocket when travelling. Useful quotations are jotted down, phrases and words not hitherto in their vocabulary are added to improve word power. They read avidly, all to keep up to date with world events and opinion.

To be a really good public speaker you must know the arguments of your opponents. Collecting opposing views to your own is more important than collating material to which you are already converted.

Even for light-hearted speaking, a filing system of amusing

anecdotes, even applicable jokes, is a great asset.

According to your speaking venues, a filing system can be put in operation. You can index it either in book form or in separate folders with specialised headings. We keep references under such headings as 'insurance', 'banking', 'political', 'sport', 'television', Fleet Street', 'showbusiness', and so on, so that if we are addressing an audience primarily interested in one of these subjects, we can immediately turn up a few apposite remarks or anecdotes in their world.

We have to be wary that what we have filed away is relatively new or something we have concocted from recent newspaper reports. To file away a joke about banking which might be fifty years old will be more or less useless as anyone in that profession will certainly have already heard it!

Unless one is expert in the subject, it is better, at light-hearted functions anyway, to avoid it altogether and provide contrast to the other experts on their feet. Simply because you are addressing a tennis club dinner does not mean you must strive to concentrate entirely on the game, especially if you are not conversant with its intricacies. If they had wanted a tennis 'ace' to address them they would not have asked you in the first place. But you can provide a change of mood, a diversion which helps the evening go along entertainingly.

It is a simple enough ploy. You state at the outset you know little or nothing of the subject, indeed you are a rabbit at tennis, or whatever the theme is, and proceed to debunk your own efforts on the courts. Then you explain your interests are elsewhere – and tell the audience about them! If you are not only informative but entertaining, they will find you a refreshing change.

Plagiarism

One should not file away extracts from other speakers' material unless you know for sure they are general quotations usable by anybody who chooses. But if that speaker has created his material himself, worked on it personally to present it his way, it is grossly unethical to steal it. The only possible outlet you would have is actually acknowledging him in your speech when you use his words. But there are plagiarists in the speaking game as there are in showbusiness.

However, the risk of being unmasked is great. There have been instances when a speaker, especially at social functions, has ruthlessly pilfered another man's speech almost in its entirety, and then one day finds himself on the same bill as the true creator! If he is faced with the problem of speaking *before* the true author his dilemma is whether to continue with the plagiarism and suffer the ultimate scorn or plead a headache and hurry from the room!

In some cases, a culprit has brazened it out and gone ahead with the 'lifted' speech in defiance of the glowering author seated near him. And when that man's turn eventually came he made an entirely different speech, giving scathing reasons for so doing, such as 'the previous speaker must have heard me before somewhere'. Although furious that his best lines have been stolen, he is experienced enough to change his material at will.

Often these speech pirates will arrogate that once someone has spoken in public there is no copyright, that it is anybody's for the asking. That layman's logic is often applied in these cases, but entirely misses the point that they have tried to pass off another's work *as their own*. Such pirates, if they ever get on professional speaking circuits, soon get struck off.

Plagiarism can boomerang in another way. The copyist speaks at a function at which the real author had addressed only a few weeks before. So the *bon mots* and neat turns of phrase are met with stony silence as they have all been heard before – and in the same order! Another wicked aspect is when the poor hardworking speaker who has created a good talk finds himself making it *after* a plagiarist has appeared. Once he is aware that the audience have heard it all before, he soon finds out who the thief is! And takes action.

A genuine speaker using good material need never imitate other speakers. Trying to get the same result from another man's lines is to assume that you have the same personality as he, which is almost certainly not the case. All public speakers must remember that they have an individual style of their own. No two people, even if making identical speeches, would present them in the same way. And the one who would do it best would undoubtedly be the speaker who originally designed it in his own image and style. Any counterfeiter would have to 'act' it.

Many such copyists have begun public speaking with the wrong concept. They see themselves as successful 'orators' long before they have ever analysed what they intend to say. The 'act' of public speaking attracts them – imparting information may not even be in their thoughts. The vanity is harmless enough to begin with, rather like a person who proclaims 'I could write a book on my experiences' but rarely ever does. However as public speaking is more accessible than writing, some tackle it in plagiaristic ways.

You must have strong personal subject matter to be a success. It means you can be a bit of a journalist or reporter with a nose for news and have a hint of a novelist in setting scenes by your words in interesting form. However tempted you might be to 'lift' another speaker's clever lines endeavour all you can to be yourself using your own creative ability. Once you have had some material of your own flagrantly 'lifted', you will appreciate this section of the book very deeply indeed!

Sources of supply

Much will depend upon your form of public speaking. Not every one of us develops into a speaker for all seasons. For those who wish to limit their speaking to business meetings, conferences, seminars or committees all within the confines of their occupation will collate material entirely relevant to that purpose. Obviously the vast majority of information you need for that will be easily accessible. But when you find that you are being asked to address audiences beyond your purely commercial or personal interests, then you will have to broaden your material and gather it from more general or topical sources.

It is fascinating how innocently you can find yourself involved in public speaking well beyond your original orbit or intention. You join a sports club and find yourself listed to propose a toast at the annual dinner. You move to a new district and find yourself involved in community interests. You become a parent and are involved in the school parents' association and so on.

Study local newspapers and ask questions round the district. Casual conversation with established shopkeepers is a mine of information. As a householder, too, you will be watchful of local authorities. Being articulate in such matters, having a voice of experience brings great respect from town councillors! Indeed one day you may join them.

The secret of good speaking is delivering your information with a clear mind. Insecurities come from an inability to think, uncluttered by side-issues, in one particular channel at a time. The concentration of so many people bobs about like a cork in the sea. The cost in time and money of sub-standard receptiveness is staggering. The public speaker in the serious sectors of life is inevitably hampered by their hearers' limited knowledge of the law, of arithmetic to appreciate economic problems and a general apathy towards helping themselves. They rely upon experienced mouthpieces to take up their causes. Many, of course, are victims of unalterable circumstances but others are content to be looked after as a right. Yet you still have to be prepared to enlighten them, to improve their lot.

Gathering material is extremely exciting. You will find new dimensions in your thinking and develop a personal knack in compiling information, your attitude to both speaking and listening changing almost entirely. One skill you will acquire is that of reconstructing items into different patterns of presentation so that the same material can be used to suit diverse audiences.

For example, an anecdote might be told in one of, perhaps, four ways, depending upon whom you are addressing. The pay-off will be identical but, by highlighting various features specific to different venues such as changing characters from male to female or altering the location in which the incident was originally set, you can make the same story applicable to, say, a women's club, an all-male rotary or sports association, a student gathering or a commercial company dinner. Thus, the same anecdote, with subtle changes, can sound personally intimate and special to each audience. It is such a simple exercise yet few seem to think of it and still tell the same old anecdote, word for word, to everybody!

Read novels and biographies all you can, especially those containing much dialogue. Not only does this improve your vocabulary but will assist you in forms of presentation. Stories about people are invaluable. Do not of course 'lift' chunks from an author's work, otherwise you might run into copyright problems, but absorb the characterisation. The spirit of a speech should be humanitarian so the more you understand people the better.

Above all, in gathering material, study conversation and take part in it as often as you can, especially with strangers. Beware of dominating the dialogue yourself, so that you personally learn nothing save to hear, once again, your own now familiar thoughts. Be prepared to ask questions rather than immediately take the initiative. It may make you feel good that people find your dialogue interesting but be sure to extract some value from theirs as well!

Often in conversation someone experienced relates an anecdote which may service you as a 'quotable quote'. Be sure you have the facts right and ask if you can use it in public. No one could stop you of course but it is an act of responsibility to seek permission. But few people will refuse if indeed they are stating a fact and will be flattered that you find their comment so worthwhile.

Use a thesaurus to find alternative words to the more obvious. Too often speakers are content with a minimal vocabulary, repeating basics like 'good', 'bad', 'nice', 'nasty', 'quick', 'slow', without ever deviating from them. A thesaurus will give you dozens more alternatives which will add power and subtlety to your speeches. You compliment your audiences with more interesting and colourful words and will certainly be more entertaining. If your subject is, say, by force of instructional circumstances, on the dull side, you can lift it into vitality with a good varied vocabulary. This is also essential when making a lighter social speech where entertainment is paramount. A good vocabulary is the keynote, too, to handling subjects outside your normal line.

One of us, when assisting the Girl Guides Association in London on their Public Speaking Proficiency Badge course, suggested the following vocabulary test. Each student was to be given a picture postcard view and asked to stand and describe it to the small audience who had not, themselves, seen it. Each had a couple of minutes to explain its details in their own words, without time to consider it beforehand.

While some might be content with 'a blue sky' others could go further ... 'a *pale* blue sky'. 'A stone castle' might be better described as 'a *grey* stone castle' and from the mere mention of 'a tower', others could improve it to 'a round tower'. Extemporisation like this is useful training for vocabulary especially if a student obtains perspective into the bargain, e.g. 'a grey stone castle with a *central* round tower in the *middle distance*, and green fields *beyond*....' From that attention to detail the audience could almost draw the scene for themselves.

It is these simple but finer points which make a speech outstanding. You are setting up a mental picture for your audience without over-elaboration and it is the difference between a flat colourless speech and a vital interesting one. Some speeches, of course, do not demand much additional detail, but nevertheless always bear in mind that you should entertain if you can, however much you are disciplined by the subject. Naturally, you avoid over-presenting a theme so that you 'wax poetical' beyond its correct interpretation. By all means use your imagination – but not your fantasies!

So gather and store away every snippet of information you can. Many speakers use the ploy of opening their discourse with: 'I saw in the paper yesterday ...' and go straight into a 'quote'. It can be either a serious observation or light-hearted. Even a misprint! But from it the speaker gets off the mark and proceeds to enlarge upon it. It is a useful scheme in early speaking when not knowing how to start presents problems to speakers especially when not bound by a special theme.

When you gain more experience you will also become adept at ad-libbing on references from immediately previous speakers. 'Miss Smith said in her splendid address just now that we males do not understand the lady's viewpoint ...' and so on. Such a development is good speaking because such teamwork is the sort of continuity audiences enjoy. Some lesser speaker, unable to cope with this form of ad-lib, often falls short in an evening of several speakers because his speech is too isolated and lacks harmony with the rest. Of course, if the others have all been deadly dull there are times when such a speaker is justified in trying to stand alone!

But you will never be dull if you seek material diligently. It is all a matter of saying to yourself: 'I speak in public so I must always be alert for information'. Information is the life blood of a good speech. Your audience want to hear something to their advantage but will appreciate it even more if you distil your knowledge entertainingly.

5

Putting your Speech on Paper

The first rough

Start by jotting down, in no particular order for the moment, the points you intend to make in your speech. Much depends upon the nature of your theme of course; it may well dictate its own running order of development by an unchangeable logical sequence. However in social or forms of academic or political speaking, the position of the various points may have to be considered carefully as to where they appear in your speech to the best advantage.

So, first, you make a list of the material you want to use. It can consist of points of order, arguments for and against, anecdotes, or even jokes, which illustrate a point, compromises, quotations of other people's views on the subject, the analysis of them, any advice or warnings you wish to pass on, and so on.

If you should be proposing or replying to a toast with names of people involved, list them and make sure they are correct by checking with the organisers. Telephone or write to find out any particulars you lack to do the task properly. Speakers too lazy to bother often offend by omitting or wrongly quoting individuals in an important speech. People who give their services voluntarily or assist in the development of a project may or may not be magnanimous if you forget to mention their personal contribution – but it is only fitting that if you are responsible for commending or thanking persons, that you are certain no one has been left out.

In a commercial speech to offend in this way would be entirely self-destructive. With modern pressures the more team-work you can infuse, the easier lies the road ahead. Even if, unintentionally, you omit a reference of this kind, you may, by implication, be taking all the credit. Those present who know it is not the case will correct you – and this could count against your integrity. Nerves might cause omissions and a quick apology soothes ruffled feelings – but the real reason is usually poor speech preparation by speakers impatient to get on with it and not surveying it on sufficiently broad a canvas.

The procedure is simple. You set your mind fully on the personalities and organisation involved, e.g. the chairman or president, the secretary, the treasurer, the promotor, the entrepreneur, the producer and even perhaps some of their assistants. Think back along the progress of the project or occasion, forgetting yourself entirely, and build up a team picture of people involved, not forgetting of course the previous speaker to whom you may be replying, until you have covered everyone within your speaking brief. If it is a dinner and your job is to thank the organisers, you may well want to include the chef or hotel manager in your appreciation. This tactful approach is not currying favours, it is merely courtesy which must be a characteristic inbred in every public speaker.

This first rough list is collated from notes you have made at random at various times when mulling over the prospect of writing the speech. Now gathered up you can begin to sort them – all facts, names and items into....

The running order

This second phase is to put your points in the best sequence. If you are replying to a previous speaker then you must acknowledge him or her immediately you rise to your feet. His words can be discussed in the first paragraph or even later in the speech, but always pay him or her the courtesy of recognition in your opening remarks.

A good speech must be like a short story – have a beginning, a middle and an end. And when brevity is of the utmost importance especially in commercial speaking, you will be wise to follow the old adage of bringing the start and finish as close together as possible! However in social speaking you are often required to provide light relief which is rarely the case in business, scientific or political channels, so there is greater latitude. But if your speech does depend on your audience absorbing vital information, you will not risk cluttering their mind with irrelevancies.

Your opening words should engender interest. This is particularly important if you are a stranger to your audience. You have, in effect, to establish yourself by capturing the room's undivided attention. As you rise the audience will be considering you 'visually' – but once you begin to speak your appearance becomes secondary for it is what you *say* which counts from then on. So your opening words must be warm and friendly, but never slick.

When commencing a speech, a long preamble or explanation must be avoided at all costs. Never sound as if you are seeking excuses for being on your feet; not, of course, unless you choose to deal with your own inability to cope in a humorous style, a well-known but still useful ploy to get off the mark in social speaking. But that approach must suit your style and personality and, even then, never be dragged out.

Beginning in a rambling style, seemingly uncertain and ultra-modest, will irritate the audience. Often this hesitant opening sets the audience's mood and, even when you warm to your task later and get to the real point of your speech, the room remains still coldly unreceptive.

In early speaking never set yourself a complicated opening, something that demands experience to handle. Many try gimmicky tricks to get under way but, in the early speeches, the best way of defeating nerves is to forget any feelings of inferiority and begin resolutely and sturdily ... 'ladies and gentlemen, I have to propose the toast of ...' or 'my subject tonight is ...'. A firm, completely concise opening sentence gives you confidence and is crystal clear as to intention. Some speakers are on their feet sometimes for over five minutes uttering mock-modest explanations in a confused prologue before getting down to their basic brief.

Remember always that opening a speech is also getting yourself 'off the ground', so the simpler it is, the less likely any initial nerves will show. Even the most experienced suffer some tension when they rise – so they never give themselves tongue-twisting statements or complex sentence formations until they are well under way. In any case never risk baffling an audience with your initial statements; they have to ease into listening to you as well, so the unsophisticated beginning is best for both of you.

When speech writing try as much as possible to avoid the obvious clichés. Aim to be original if you can. Too many speakers, new to the public scene feel obliged to tread the well-worn paths, parroting phrases already stale in the ears of many past generations. 'Unaccustomed as I am ...' 'who needs no introduction ...', 'it gives me great pleasure ...' (you might be nervous thus making that an obvious lie!), 'I am deeply conscious of the honour....' New speakers sometimes do not think of replacing these hoary statements, perhaps considering them to be such a part of a conventionalised, formal drill that they must be included in public speaking.

Clichés are harmless enough and, if there is no alternative, you will not offend by using them. But such lofty old-time phrasing often clashes when fused with the modern idiom ... 'It is my great honour and privileged duty to inform you all gathered here on this auspicious occasion in the history of our distinguished club that there will be bingo and disco in the scout hut next Thursday....'

Constructing your speech in correct order

You know your subject and you have collated all you wish to say about it. Now to sort it out in a presentable order. Untutored speakers are apt to consider their own self-portrait when preparing a speech rather than think of it in relation to pleasing the audience. Speakers, to be successful, must be constantly thinking beyond themselves both in writing and rehearsing speeches. You need to say to yourself ... 'Would I find this speech enjoyable if I were listening to it rather than delivering it? Am I going to sound really as interesting as I hope I am?'

You have to be your own ruthless critic.

No intelligent speaker ever blames his audience. Without them he would not be speaking at all and his duty must be to please them if he hopes they will please him! They must enjoy his speech, otherwise he will not enjoy making it. There are of course some thick-skinned speakers who will drone on as if entirely divorced from audiences, apparently not caring whether they were there or not.

The necessary ingredients are 'interest' and 'entertainment' whatever the subject. So, when preparing your speech points you must strive to get the best balance possible. No good using your best stuff at the opening and tailing off after a bright start. You have to maintain interest throughout. This means juggling your material, assessing the strong and not so strong points and alternating them so that the speech does not flag into boredom. Conversely a dull opening will not be compensated by a bright finish. If bored at the opening, the audience will no longer be fully receptive by the time you reach your best material. As a thriller writer aims to end his chapters with cliff hanger suspense, so you, in a more moderated form of construction, must aim to keep your speech stimulating.

The four phases of speech construction

1. The opening When you rise to your feet you must ensure you have the right form of address ... 'Ladies and gentlemen' is the obvious one but VIPs may be present who take precedence ('Your Highness, my Lord Mayor'). Also you may be replying to an individual speaker so that the opening address might be 'Mr Chairman, Mr Smith, ladies and gentlemen....' So do check with the organisers beforehand.

Then follow with a concise reference to your subject or reason for speaking. The announcement from a toastmaster or menu information may tell the audience but nevertheless make sure the audience know your purpose. Announcements can be blurred by bad acoustics or a coughing bout from the front. So ensure they know from you personally what your subject is.

2. Setting your scene   It could be that your subject has already caused comment or is controversial. Then, again, your audience may be completely in the dark about it and need enlightenment. There may be a debatable division of opinion which needs to be ironed out before you can get to the crux of the subject. Therefore you anticipate these queries in the audience's mind and cover them to the best of your ability. In other words, you are clearing a path for yourself so that the way is free for your treatment to come.

You can possibly include, at this stage, a reference to your own qualifications – or, in a light-hearted speech, your lack of them! – to merit your being there to discuss the subject. This second phase ensures that the audience knows exactly who you are and why the speech is in your charge. Depending upon your subject you set the stage accordingly, putting all the initial facts to your audience to guide them when you reach the meat of your subject. Anecdotes pertinent to this development are extremely useful. Illustrations of ignorance or intolerance of it, misconceptions, misunderstandings or a witty example of its value all help. Laughter, within the subject, is valuable at this point. It sets the tone. The audience will realise you are also entertaining and the listening will remain acute. A relevant quotation from an expert is also worth inserting at this stage.

3. The main plot   Now that the audience is clear about your subject and its various aspects, you give them the main ingredients of the plot. You analyse your subject fully, voice opinion, give advice and suggestions, diagnose and cure any malaise connected with it. You include any characters involved – especially in social speeches – and again use anecdote and example. How to do something correctly is easy to explain but it is the anecdote of someone who fails to take the proper steps which sinks into the audience's minds best. They laugh and remember the warning at the same time. If you want people to follow any special instruction, the safest way of getting through to them is to tell them how *not* to do it!

One cannot anticipate in writing a speech what earlier speakers will say on the subject before you but if there have been references to it you might well include your observations upon them at this point.

You reach your climax, your highlight. You stress your viewpoint be it a personal or a logical conclusion, perhaps ending on your funniest anecdote or most telling aspect of your speech.

4. *The conclusion* If your subject requires it, give a brief resumé of what you have said, reiterating the important points, stressing warnings. In a social speech you would mention any acknowledgements at this point, giving thanks to any individuals concerned. Then you thank your audience for their attention – and sit down.

So, when compiling your speech from your jottings, sort them into the most applicable phase of the four. Once you have each one segregated you can then further adjust them into their best order within that phase so that the best effect is derived from them. You study weight of impact, relativity and balance. In other words, do not put all the eggs in one basket so that your talk begins well but fades at the end with less entertaining or relevant material. Remember, each phase, barring the last, should have a climax to which you build up. You have to maintain interest throughout, interweaving perhaps light relief with serious considerations. Aim not to get bogged down with data ... sew together a patchwork quilt of alternate quiet and bright colours all you can.

Technical talks often fall into place in a natural progression. But in social speaking a particular sequence is not always self-explanatory. It is up to you to plot the course of each phase. Even more vital is the political field where you have to be extremely careful to prepare a speech on an ascending scale of importance.

Avoid, if you can, prefacing the last phase with 'In conclusion ...'. Often it is a sign that some speakers are going to double the length of their talk! The most significant ending to a speech is that 'thank you' before you sit down. No need to particularly herald the fact you are reaching the end. Certainly avoid the learner's 'well, I think that's all I have to say ...'!

Bridging links

Having arranged your points in the best order, there comes the question of joining them together. So you need bridging links, sentences which take you smoothly from one point to another or signpost changes of subject or aspect. You have to aim for fluidity, good smooth continuity. You cannot abruptly switch from point to point without the speech sounding staccato and abrupt.

Bridging links are simple but it is surprising how many speakers omit them in their speech notes and so have to resort to 'ers' and 'ums'. Sometimes only one word serves as a bridging link – 'conversely', 'paradoxically', 'alternatively', 'again'.

Make the speech flow as a complete entity, not a series of isolated facts strung together with such phrases as 'which brings me to ...'. 'next I want to talk about ...' or worse 'which reminds me of ...' when what has just been said bears no relationship whatsoever with what comes next! Bridging gaps marry the points rather than leaving them completely divorced from each other, thus causing bald gaps in delivery.

The art of public speaking lies partly in this easy transition. It is relatively easy to emphasise your main items but much of the impact will be lost if they are not bridged smoothly. As a story flows on paper easing from one situation into another, so should a speech.

A complete change of subject needs a pause and a special bridging link to herald it. The single word helps here, or if you want to be more precise you can say 'Now a completely new line of approach ...', 'A different point of view is ...', 'There is, however, another aspect....' There is no need to labour a change of subject provided you pause and give the audience one sentence to indicate the new tack.

In science, technology or commerce, economy of time may not allow much latitude in bridging gaps. When speed of information is of the essence, more abrupt changes of subject may be necessary so the 'one word' bridging gap is valuable. In such cases your audience will be, to a certain extent at least, already familiar with your subject so the social speech technique will not be required. But if your audience is taking notes, longer bridging gaps are necessary to allow them to absorb each valuable point.

As you gain experience you will indulge in certain improvisations of your own according to the function at which you are speaking but good bridging gaps, make-weight as they may seem, mark the expert from the learner.

Putting your speech on paper

For beginners the best way of tackling this job is to phrase it as you might in a letter. Informality is the keynote of a social speech, while sheer facts dominate a business or scientific talk. You do not need to be a qualified author to write a speech. You have, however to bear two vital points in mind – your own personality and pleasing the audience. So, your assessment of yourself and your ability must be an honest one.

Keeping to your time limit

Use a stop watch or the second hand of your ordinary watch and check, by reading aloud your speech, that you are within the limit set by the organisers. If they have asked for ten minutes, they expect you to respect that wish. Far too many speakers ignore this courtesy. So a well-planned evening becomes a scurry for the last buses and trains because one or two speakers bore them for half an hour each. By speaking too long you will not only ruin the organisers' schedule, but also use up a lot more material of your own which you could well use on other occasions, or even on a 'repeat' date at the same venue.

If you get a reputation for overrunning your time, you may be left out of future plans. So keep to the time granted you; as you progress this will be in your favour and by the time you get VIP speaking status they will allot you the last speaking spot with perhaps twenty minutes to half an hour to yourself. And how will you feel if the first speaker proceeds to use fifteen minutes of that by over-running? It will be your lot then, to speak to a fast-emptying room as people rush to catch the last available transport home without even being able to have a final drink in the now closed bar!

Use of slang

Only use slang terms sparingly. Then they can be vivid and effective – but compile a speech mainly comprised of idiomatic or loose phrases of an off-beat nature and you will not have much vocabulary to play with. Some subjects may be quite wrong for slang but a speaker might use it purposely to denote his or her own personality. That can alienate an audience very quickly! However there is no taboo on slang terms in public speaking. What you have to consider though is whether it suits your subject – and your audience. It is no good calling them old-fashioned when you find your trendy dialogue has not pleased them. Your job is to gain their approval of your speech. You will be the biggest loser if you fail to reach the standard they desire.

Being too racy is a common fault among early speakers. They think it enhances their image and often use slang to cover nerves thinking such casual speaking will give an impression of relaxation. Then an odd swear word is slipped in to show what 'with-it' person he or she is. It rarely works and there is more risk of offence than gaining applause. It might be accepted if the audience knows you personally – but that will not always be the case.

Slang terms are best used in the dialogue you portray in anecdotes. You are relating a true story and so the terms used are fact. Most experienced speakers only use slang in that context – so achieving a vivid contrast to their own personal remarks. Thus when a single slang term is used by an erudite speaker, it adds to his or her creative ability for, by using it so sparingly, they gain added impact. But sprinkle a speech with obscenities and 'in' terms and you risk the speech falling flat. Slang actually becomes more dated than normal, clear cut speech and mostly it gives the impression of someone trying too hard.

Vocabulary

A good vocabulary is one of the most important factors in public speaking. We have suggested you avoid threadbare clichés and strike out on a more personal approach, so that what you say really does sound like you and your normal conversation. Yet do not descend to the limited daily dialogue. Avoid 'it's fantastic', 'great', 'super', 'magic', all the exaggerations of modern optimism.

Keep your vocabulary reasonably simple and keep your dictionary and thesaurus handy as you write a speech. Thus you can find alternative words for the obvious; not, of course, of a mannered, pseudo-intellectual nature which could cause you to be dubbed pretentious.

Many variations of common-place words are well-known to you but they do not always spring to mind when preparing a speech. Study the variations in a thesaurus as bedside reading. '*Quick*' is commonplace – but there is also 'rapid', 'active', 'intelligent', 'skilful' or even 'irascible'. '*Quiet*' is obvious – but why not use 'calm', 'restful', 'dissuade' (in the context of 'quietening down') or 'leisurely'. '*Slow*' might be more interestingly implied by 'tardy', 'moderate', 'inactive', 'wearisome', 'dull' or 'inert'.

'*Noise*' is often expressed in speeches – but you also have a choice of 'sound', 'din', 'loud', 'clatter', 'roar', 'uproar', 'racket', 'fracas', 'blast', 'blare', 'deafen', 'stun', and many more variations in noun, adjective or adverb form all far more explicit in variation than mere 'noise'. Each alternative has a special degree of meaning which can lift your statement from the obvious to the interesting.

Increasing your word power is half the advantage of preparing a speech. You must have a sound working vocabulary to express yourself well in public A limited vocabulary means restricted self-expression, leading to frustration, intolerance and lack of imagination and creative power. Speakers limited in vocabulary have to resort to repetition – and that soon bores the listener.

Avoid repeated phrases like 'didn't I?', 'wasn't I?' and 'OK?'

and 'you know what I mean' when finishing a sentence. It may sound informal but it also denotes a pathetic need for reassurance. Mostly people copy these 'fashions' from television characters and even some screen script writers have put such phrases into Victorian and Edwardian mouths although they would never have used them. Constant repetition however does serve to implant them into more shallow, uncreative minds. These time-wasting, conversational expressions should never be used in public speaking. Try, always, to sound original – and new!

The final draft of a speech

You have verified all your facts, you have checked names and you know that you must have a beginning, middle and end for your speech. You want to keep it within your own limitations, your own true character orbit although each successive speech will add a dimension to your future ability. Do not set yourself an impossible task which may seem surmountable at rehearsal but, when initial nerves beset you on the first occasion you face an audience, you find that you have too difficult a speech construction to handle confidently. No one would deny enterprise but sometimes impatience makes ambition exceed ability in early days.

So design a speech that you can give within a safety margin. You know your time limit is say ten minutes and you will write with that in mind. You will allot for the first phase one minute, the second phase perhaps two, third phase six and last phase one. There are your ten minutes and you have a correct balance.

With the countless subjects available for public speakers it is difficult to set down an example which will apply most generally. However we will take 'motoring' as the theme and make a 'break down' of its various aspects as one might in preparation for a speech.

First Phase: Introduction and information to audience that you will speak on, say, 'motoring'. State your qualifications generally. Use anecdote to illustrate your suitability or experience.
Second Phase: Setting your scene. Difficulties of motoring,

garaging, parking, petrol stations, freeway problems, other motorists, speeding fines, traffic wardens, relationships with police and highway patrols, maintenance of vehicles, the family car, the business model, the commercial truck (the prestige and the practical).

Third Phase: The main plot. Advice, the causes and cures of traffic problems, the motor industry itself, and motoring needs for various sections of commerce and family leisure. New roads as against conservation of the countryside. Include anecdotes giving examples of these points.

Fourth Phase: The conclusion. A brief summary of main points and mention of any part the audience can play to help the problems. Then into brief tributes to any helpers or organisers. Say 'thank you' and resume your seat.

You will be able to adjust that format to the various subjects which will come your way, either in light-hearted or educational public speaking. Your mind soon becomes practised in sorting out aspects of your main theme and develops an understanding of the important facts, the semi-important and the more minor aspects so that you will construct your speeches in a balanced way.

What you have to avoid is getting bogged down by a single aspect of a subject. You have to think round it, beyond it, to include all its associated themes, every possible permutation, the people concerned with it, its effects on those it employs, money involved, future development, past success or failures, etc. Every subject has links beyond its root.

Where new speakers find speech writing difficult is not thinking beyond those roots up to the branches, leaves, blossoms, fruit – and birds' nests – in the tree above!

Studying a speech before rehearsal

Once fully written out, you should, to some extent, be able to judge the audience's reaction to your speech. You have to be candid. Are you taking a risk in any section which might displease? Are you over-personalising yourself at the expense of the subject? Read it through carefully with the audience in mind, rather than yourself. Not easy – but try and judge it from their viewpoint. Will they share your views or enjoy your style of presentation? Is there any chance you may spoil the occasion by some error of judgment?

If you are preparing a commercial speech within your employment you must consider your brief in depth. You have something to 'sell' so your facts must be right and every aspect expected by the audience must be covered. Reports or statements round an executive table must be made succinctly. As to what additional opinions or comments you offer beyond the facts, that entirely depends on your position in the organisation. Gratuitous remarks beyond his brief, however well intended, have been the downfall of many an up-and-coming employee!

Only you will know whether or not your expertise is required over and above your basic statement. Much better in the early days to make the report concisely, allow others to discuss it and then ask, through the chair, if you may comment. Some 'instant success' types reject such protocol, and blaze away, bull at a gate, in the mistaken notion that speed is *always* essential. It is not. If by such tactics you induce hostility by trying to railroad your ideas through, much more time is actually wasted.

In commercial speaking there may be no place – or time – for light relief. However if you do intend using it, make sure it is quite appropriate to the subject and occasion rather than a digression just to enhance your personality. Otherwise you may well spoil a good technical talk by sounding flippant. Combining humour with serious instruction needs a lot of experience to make it harmonise – especially if time is short.

In a political speech the running order of points is anyone's guess. But you will still need that strong opening, powerful middle and big finish. Preaching to your own converted is simple enough – there will be applause and cries of 'hear hear' and standing ovations. It is when faced with opposition that the test comes. You must sound fluent and, above all, be economical in a speech. Any hesitations will be considered a sign of weakness, any uncertainties will wreck your cause. Simple uncomplicated sentences must be used so that, if you are heckled, you can easily remember and repeat the point.

Political audiences judge your speaking talent by what you stand for. They will only consider you a good speaker if in what you say there is promise of good things for them!

The political arena is a tough one – a sense of humour is invaluable but has to be used extremely cautiously. What may be funny to your own party can be an insult to the opposition. It is a question of the degree to which you take it. So take care in looking for laughter in politics.

The social speech to a well-wined and dined community is vastly different – and strangely enough, the most difficult speech to write. You have far fewer guidelines than in commerce or other fields which have natural progressions. Often your subject in the social field is just a vague toast like 'The Guests'. Once you have listed them and lauded their qualities, it is then up to you to embellish the speech entertainingly.

Without any firm foundation you have to be inventive. It is not good speaking to go off at a tangent of isolated funny jokes to fill the gap. You still have to keep within the context of your brief. But you can tell jokes or, better still, anecdotes, which have the added advantage of being authentic, about the jobs the guests you are toasting hold. This maintains continuity.

If they be a banker, insurance official or a lawyer, then once you have completed your personal references to them, with a little imagination you can anecdote about other bankers, insurance officials, lawyers you have known or heard about. This gets your light relief in harmoniously with the subject. The bridging links are simple.... 'Our lawyer friend here tonight is certainly not like the one I heard of who ...' and then into anecdote or joke about the legal profession. Naturally you keep the humour good-natured and without insult to the three guests, but merely use their occupations to build up the speech entertainingly.

You will find it far easier to compile a social speech if you think through the brief rather than hurry over it and end the speech with entirely foreign material. Even the problems of preparing a speech make a good and amusing stop-gap subject for social occasions!

Mention of family or children is always a safe bet with a social audience. If a previous speaker has mentioned his or her domestic life, you can use that pivot to mention your own. Anecdotes, especially against yourself, as troubled parent or victim of some kiddies' con trick, is a winner. You hurt nobody else and, if the situation is one in which the audience can visualise itself, you will always get laughs.

Social speeches should be designed to enhance the occasion – uplift it, enrich it. Never be tempted to put a damper on any aspect, unless it is vitally necessary for the discipline of the occasion. In any event, it is unwise to use the social platform to talk on extremely sombre subjects or issue dire warnings. The audience are there to enjoy themselves in an escapist mood. They do not want propaganda of any sort.

Write the speech out including the bridging links, in complete form. This helps you to use a stop watch on it to make sure you have not extended your allotted length. If the speech is typed use treble spacing so that insertions and corrections can be made. It is surprising when reading it aloud to yourself, how many more apt phrases and new aspects spring to mind as it jells into a complete 'story'. But if your speech is running true to length you will have to cut or shorten other lines to add new items.

It is a question of studying the importance of the subject, assessing how seriously it should be taken and what entertainment you can infuse into it, within your own personality, without taking liberties or chances on questionable material. You will have a good idea of what sort of audience to expect. If they are intelligent, they will not want verbal custard pies. If they are a sports club on a Saturday night binge, they will want their humour broad. So handle your subject as much as possible with the anticipated audience in mind, always keeping within the boundaries of your natural personality. Good-natured, enthusiastic audiences are apt to over-stimulate new speakers, tempting them to become 'instant' extroverts. The more repose you can maintain, the better will you be enjoyed.

We reiterate – compile the speech in the mood of writing a letter to a friend so that it contains your own true personality.

Keep the style conversational rather than as an acting role, but of course, omit all those useless expressions of daily dialogue – 'd'you know what we mean?'!

6

Speech Rehearsal and Use of Notes

Committing a speech completely to memory might be an asset in early days of a speaking career but it should not become a habit. A very important speech affecting your future not only as a speaker but in other vital aspects of your life might well merit 'learning by heart' to ensure success. There are, too, ritualistic occasions in freemasonry and societies with traditional formats which may require verbatim learning, so, if you move in such circles, you must be prepared to fully learn lines.

The danger of learning a speech off by heart is that it can sound stilted. Concentration upon exactitude can affect repose and presentation. On highly formal occasions certain addresses are read in proclamation form. But never read a whole speech if you can possibly avoid it. Some speakers do. Their heads are lowered constantly over a script so that there is no facial expression, no smile and no eye movement to take in various corners of the room. A speech under these circumstances is utterly devoid of personality.

Your aim is to reach a stage when your memory has stored up the speech sufficiently well to need nothing more than headings on notes to know what comes next. Then, if your speech does contain a section which demands a guaranteed accuracy of statement, that portion *can* be read to avoid mistakes. But in public speaking in all fields, audiences prefer the semi-ad-lib delivery of a speaker who refers to notes only occasionally.

Never be ashamed of using notes. The clergyman is a good example. He remembers the marriage ceremony, but he still has the Book there in case of a sudden mental black-out. Experienced actors will confirm this. Even after playing a role hundreds of times, there can be a moment when their mind goes blank. The prompter is taken by surprise – but usually other actors on stage will quickly bring the lines back. It has even been known in opera when a singer has 'dried' and other quick-thinking performers have taken up the lines. But you, a public speaker, have no company of players on stage with you, there is no one in the prompt corner, no television autocue; you are a solo performer – so have your notes ready.

In early speaking it is advisable to commit as much to memory as possible – but, on the night, rather than a full script, use notes to keep you on the right track. Your aim is to master the ability to look down at your notes, see a block lettered heading and know in your mind immediately what you intend to say on that particular item. When that section is exhausted, you again glance down at your next heading and proceed to discuss that. Even if you are completely familiar with your speech this method ensures that you are not 'thrown' if an unexpected interruption upsets concentration.

The use of the 'heading' technique is valuable for many reasons. If time is pressing you can cut portions of a speech by passing over less important headings and still be able to take up your theme fluently a stage or two further on. It also allows you to insert last-minute additions necessitated by remarks from other speakers or information gathered just prior to the event.

If you have learned a speech by heart such additions or omissions are most difficult to make. A remark made by a previous speaker invites a reply from you and you have to wrack your brains to know exactly where to insert it – and still remember what follows. Cutting something out – possibly because another speaker has already covered the subject before you rise – is even more difficult as it will often ruin the fluency. You have to posses a photographic mind to handle such a situation and few are that lucky.

. (Incidentally, 'learning by heart' stems from the Latin 'apprehendere per chorum', a 'chorus' repetitive system chanted by pupils committing mathematical tables and other scholastic information firmly in their minds. But the French managed to mis-translate 'chorum' into 'apprendre par *coeur*' so 'learning by *heart*' entered the English vocabulary.)

Cue cards

For your notes use postcards or, if you want a slightly larger size for your vision, cut oblongs from thin cardboard of the type often used for stiffeners in shirt boxes. Never use flimsy paper for speech notes. It will rustle into the microphone when turned and inevitably droop down out of eyeline just when you need a reference most!

Mark these cards with cue headings for each progressive stage of your speech, using bold block lettering which can be read at stomach level. If your notes are too small for your vision at that range you will have to hold them under your chin which hampers delivery. Your card cues should be plainly visible a foot below the microphone head.

Head card 1 with name of function and date. Then, when you later file it away, should you receive an invitation to speak again to that audience, you can refer to it and give them something new. It is surprising how lax some quite eminent speakers are on this point. They will return after a couple of years and give exactly the same speech!

Number your cue cards in the top right hand corner so that, should they become disordered during your speech, they are easily sorted out without too long a pause. Make sure every card is complete in itself. Do not continue the same line of thought or heading over to another card which can cause you to juggle with them to get full information. Each heading should be a complete cue in itself so that what you intend to say on that aspect readily springs to your mind. That makes turning to card 3, say, after completing your remarks on the headings of card 2, a completely natural pause in your delivery. A normal speech can usually be summarised under headings on about four cards. Leave wide spaces between the headings so that you can insert last-minute needs occasioned by references of previous speakers or new aspects which strike you during the run-up of events before you are announced.

Changes of direction need headings and it is advisable, if you have made the speech several times before, to make any new headings in a different coloured ink so that you spot the change and do not plough on from force of habit in the old routine.

Use a separate card for any material you may want to hold in reserve. This covers references that you are uncertain whether you will need or not before you actually arrive at the venue. Perhaps a certain person might be present or a possible subject mentioned which cannot be anticipated as a certainty. So you make notes on your 'reserve' card to meet this eventuality but can ignore it if the occasion does not arise.

A further blank card is often useful for making notes upon other speeches prior to your own. However only use this if you do not wish to make insertions on your four cards. Speakers sometimes prefer to use the same four main cards over and over again and take additional references from a spare card. In the main, however, it is better to alter the four cards and rewrite a fresh set for every speech. If your cards contain only four headings each, there should be space for last minute reminders and additions.

If postcard size they fit easily in jacket pockets or handbags which allow you to study them at almost any odd leisure moment. Train or plane travel gives an excellent opportunity to familiarise yourself with a speech. The cards are not conspicuous and will be always handy for impromptu rehearsal.

Diligent rehearsal

Rehearsing a speech thoroughly is vital however boring you may find it. In early days of speaking you need all you can get for, as all experienced speakers know, it is one thing to know your words in front of a mirror but quite another to be as fluent in front of a sea of faces! The very presence of an audience is atmospheric, a humming of life which you cannot simulate at rehearsal. It is true to say that one should almost grow stale on the early speeches to ensure that, when you finally rise before an audience, you will manage to give a first class performance. Usually, anyway, stage-fright is caused by speakers' own insecurity in what they are going to say, and in being under-rehearsed. They only have a vague idea of the subject and a few hazy points jotted down, and lack format and decisive construction. If your subject is clear-cut and its exact progression firmly rooted in your mind, then the delivery of it, rather than remembering it, is your only worry. In other words, the battle is half won before you stand up.

Begin by rehearsing with your full script. It is a question of reading it through out loud, time after time. In early readings you will find you need to make a few corrections as better phrasing or new ideas are stimulated by the exercise. Once the script is completely to your satisfaction the task of committing it to memory begins. As you rehearse you will gradually find your eyes leaving the pages and you will continue for long passages without any need to refresh your mind. You have absorbed the sense of every phrase of the speech, your bridging links are smooth and economical and the speech flows well with precise timing.

What you have to master in speech-making is 'seeing' a picture in your mind so that you recreate it for your audience. You are imparting word pictures to the audience which, a split second before, have been 'visible' to yourself. Train yourself assiduously in this art. If, for example, you are recounting a personal experience, you should actually relive it in your mind and, as you talk, the characters and the backcloth of street or room in which the event took place, will come to life again behind your eyes.

This also applies to technical and commercial speeches. Your brain will 'show' you diagrammatically the progress of the problem which you then relay to the audience. Describing what the mind is creating is the true art of speech making. Certainly the best raconteurs describe what their brain 'sees' at the time, not merely what it has remembered. Each time they tell a story it lives again. Even a two line joke will evoke a brief picture.

Cultivate your mind this way. A good speech is not just words remembered in the right order but a series of colourful illustrations portrayed by the speaker for the audience to re-form in their own minds. No two versions would, if it was possible to collate them, ever be the same, but the more skilled the speaker is the closer the images would be to an over-all conception by the audience. The object in public speaking is to integrate an audience so that the nearer they are to being of one mind, the more receptive they will be.

If you were to challenge an experienced speaker as to what he 'saw' when he related an anecdote, he would surprise you with the wealth of detail he could muster ... items perhaps that he does not even mention in the delivery of it. Front doors, lamp-posts, railings, curbstones, curtains, etc, which, although irrelevant to the story, 'appeared' to him. The audience might just be told that a man and a woman have met ... but if he is telling the anecdote well, he will even 'clothe' the people himself.

Public speakers of any grade have this form of perception but some take longer than others to bring it to full fruition. Practice does it. You will know if you have it by listening to a radio play and study how you 'dress' the characters, distinguishable only by voice, who knock on unseen doors or drive invisible cars, which you will also envisage as solid objects.

When you feel familiar with your speech, discard the full script and take up the cue cards. Start rehearsing from the headings alone. You will be surprised how easy the transition is. You will feel a sudden freedom to extemporise. No longer will you be quoting the exact script but you will still make complete sense. The cue cards keep you in the right groove of the subject but your mind travels lighter. Certainly you must concentrate completely on the speech, thinking through it all the time but you will vary phrases, change vocabulary and bridging links much as you would in ordinary conversation.

Access to a tape recorder is useful but do not rush straight to it and start recording your speech after only a couple of run-throughs. Do so only when you are convinced that you have put in adequate rehearsal and are delivering the words within the allotted time. Then play it back listening for flaws, hesitations, poor pronunciation, missed pauses and lack of emphasis. Check whether you are apt to tail away towards the end of a sentence – a common fault in early speaking. Hear your pitch and be sure you are giving the audience time to digest your words fully.

Listen to your breathing. Is it even and unnoticeable or heavy and obvious? Are you trying to pack too many words into each lungful of air? If so, find a space in the sentence for a pause, a comma, colon, or semi-colon, mark it and rehearse that portion again. As we have stressed earlier there is always a tendency to speed up through anxiety to get on with the job but this over-eagerness makes a speech ragged in presentation. A tape recorder can help obviate this.

Note, too, if you expect laughter after an anecdote, that you have allowed yourself sufficient pause so as not to talk into the laugh. Of course you will not wait until the room has returned to complete silence, but speak again just when the last chuckles are fading.

Then, once you have assessed yourself from that tape, scrap it and after more rehearsal to erase errors, record again. Certainly do *not* use the earlier tape, full of mistakes, to commit the speech by ear. It might help you memorise the words but it will almost certainly implant the errors on your mind and you will learn those too!

When you feel you have reached your peak, whether you have recording facilities or not, ask a friend or two to listen to your speech. By friends we mean candid ones, not those who are not prepared to criticise for fear of offending you. Seek out, if you are able, someone already experienced in facing audiences and let them hear you. If they are true friends they will not flatter to deceive.

Many mature speakers still carry their notes although they may, when on the circuits, have made the same speech or lecture hundreds of times. This is because they have discovered that, without them to hand, something is missing from their performance, perhaps a slight inbuilt anxiety, and that they have once or twice, quite inexplicably, left out a portion. So notes in hand give you a safety margin.

Shut yourself away when you rehearse. You cannot memorise words and nuances of speech in a crowded room. Turn off radio and television sets and find complete solitude.

Always rehearse on your feet. Not pacing up and down but stock still as you will be when the big moment arrives. Keep your script – and later, your cue cards – in hand and imagine a microphone before you just below your chin. If you are lecturing and know that a lectern will be provided at your engagement, improvise that with a pile of books. Rehearse with a chair behind you, indeed begin sitting down, if your speech is of the after-lunch or dinner variety. For these events even work with a table before you.

As much as you can, after the initial memory run-throughs, give yourself as near a dress rehearsal as possible. Ladies would be advised to practise their speech in the dress they propose to wear if it might present problems. So often they have to speak wearing ball gowns at dinner/dances, and they are not always the easiest of clothing if full and flowing, so a dress rehearsal is common sense.

At these latter rehearsals use every gesture and imagine an audience out front, create a sea of faces on that blank lounge wall – and work to them. Rehearsals will not be boring if you can shut yourself away from prying eyes and caustic family comment and really let yourself go, giving correct voice projection. You do not have to rattle the pictures and ornaments but just lift your voice above ordinary conversational level without shouting. The best balance to achieve at rehearsal is to imagine you are speaking to someone about ten feet away. You would not have to yell but just raise your tone sufficiently to make them hear.

Rehearsals will not be a chore if you use your imagination – but stop short of 'hearing' roars of approval at the end! That will happen only if you have tackled the speech conscientiously, prepared to give only your best. You may find the drill boring and be tempted to trust to fate that all will be well on the night. But when you do rise, under-rehearsed, you will regret that attitude as the stumbles and line-fluffing starts. How then will you wish you had spent a little more time on rehearsal!

Speech learning soon becomes second nature with practice. Verbatim memory, as we stress, is not necessary but balanced knowledge of what you intend to say in each phase of your subject is vital. Most speakers, well versed in the art, often make the same speech but never deliver it identically at any time. The subject and points of order are consistent but the construction alters slightly every time it is delivered. That is the true enjoyment of public speaking. You are not hide-bound to a set script – only a subject. You can extemporise at will according to your audience. You become confident enough to vary vocabulary as the mood takes you, insert after-thoughts or topicalities of the moment, possibly only valid for one particular occasion. This of course demands that you still retain fluency of delivery. Once a speaker side-tracks himself and starts groping for a word and, by improvising, gets out of his depth, he loses impact.

Of course there is every excuse for hesitancy if a speaker has been dragged to his feet without previous warning. It does happen, especially if a speaker is ill and a last-minute deputy has to be found. Even under such duress, however, a practised speaker will give a good account of himself. He shrugs off his 'embarrassment' at the late request with good humour for he knows the game well enough and has some stock anecdotes up his sleeve to cover such occasions. Really he will enjoy the challenge and, however spontaneous his remarks appear, these seemingly ad-lib speakers are the most rehearsed of all! They have stored up enough material over the years to make speeches at the drop of a hat and are never lost for words.

Good descriptive speaking is an art which pleases every audience. To be told 'I could have listened to you all night' is the finest accolade a speaker can receive.

7

Humour in Public Speaking

Those in the speaking game who can raise laughter are invaluable – but they must be very astute at assessing each particular audience. The fun must be compatible with both the occasion and the subject of the speech. Comedy must arise from within the theme, and merge into the material as a cohesive advancement of the argument.

Humour is a fascinating study and an important ingredient in a speaker's repertoire but it has to be used with a keen sense of proportion. In instructional talks humour is often used to press home how *not* to perform the operation under review, so that, with the laugh at a victim's expense, knowledge of correct procedure will be absorbed by the audience. As long as the humour has a positive value in advancing the subject, it remains a very strong weapon in any speaker's armoury.

However, too many beginners see humour as the beginning-and-end of public speaking. Laughter acts upon them like a drug, giving them a feeling of power, which they dispense in a commanding manner. Do not take up public speaking as a step towards being a comedian. It will not help you until you have a precise knowledge of the vastly different techniques required in speech making.

Of course it is gratifying to hear laughter. It is a sign of audience-approval even before the final applause, reassuring to an insecure speaker, especially early on in a speech. If that laughter has been caused by fun being applied directly to the speaker's subject he is on course, doing a good job.

However there are those who will merely stand up, brush aside their speech brief and resort to a string of entirely unrelated jokes as their contribution to the occasion. It may well please their immediate pals but, in the wider and more intelligent fields of public speaking, simply reveals a complete lack of ability to communicate as an individual. There is no personal creativity, the second-hand stories are strung together haphazardly without the continuity of bridging links and are often rapped out at machine-gun rate, with self-complimentary chuckles in between. If such an extrovert is performing in cabaret, then he is justified, but if he is asked to make a speech he must take the trouble to relate his comedy to the reason for the audience being there.

It is all too common in public speaking. The speaker cannot think of anything apposite to say for the occasion so resorts to isolated jokes. Perhaps, at a very light-hearted function when the speaker is a complete novice, and does not intend speaking seriously in public, this ploy is readily forgivable but it is an 'act', not a speech and will not further his ability to impart interesting information. Those in his audience with similar 'comic' aspirations will probably 'lift' his jokes anyway by writing them on the menu!

The real danger lies when these would-be comics do not know the difference between the offensive and the inoffensive joke. Some indulge in 'blue' stories just to please a minority clique in the audience – but end up affronting the vast majority who resent paying for sub-standard speaking. What is acceptable on the night-club floor is not always appropriate for a social gathering. How often has the best man's speech at a wedding reception been in thoroughly poor taste because of dubious honeymoon gags?

Speakers using humour must, if they want to be popular, know the needs of each particular audience they address. A speaker who will flaunt dirty jokes as a sort of challenge to unsuspecting audiences is soon struck off the speaking rolls. Discomfited organisers spread the word – and those who recommended such a speaker are called to order at the next committee meeting. Sometimes it is not entirely the fault of the comic himself. Some club official may have heard him at a 'stag' party, found him hilarious and then over-enthusiastically booked him for an entirely different occasion where more sobriety and depth of speaking is required. Maybe he is expected to be versatile enough to alter his script but, instead delivers the same material. The room seethes with anger as he struggles on, finally to sit down prematurely to dead silence. He will be sullen or aggressive – putting the blame for his failure squarely on the audience.

That defence of failure to please, however, can never be justified. Whichever way you look at it any audience you face is entitled to its opinion of your contribution. It is useless to claim that the jokes have all been heard in public before. People can switch off television sets and stay away from night clubs. In a democratic world all people are entitled to have their own standards of humour. This applies not only to the 'blue' story but also to the snide remark misguidedly intended as satire but which offends instead.

Humour must be used intelligently. Take no risks with questionable material unless you are absolutely certain your audience expects it. Even then you must consider your own standing. There is no prestige if the waitresses have to be asked to leave the dining room when you stand up to speak!

We are aware that standards of humour have changed over the years. Both sex and religion are mocked in varying forms but that style is not worldwide and genuine wit and artistry are always appreciated. Tragically, there are those to whom humour is solely confined to copulation and the toilet. Unfortunately some fancy themselves as public speakers. However, being known for your reliability in your choice of material is a necessity if you are to fully succeed.

Being funny

The trouble with comedy is that it *looks* easy. One sees a comedian on stage or television and how simple it all seems! He tells a funny story – and the audience folds up hysterically. A delightful way of earning a living, thinks the layman, this is popularity on a plate. But rarely can these copyists dissect what goes into the 'gag', the timing, phrasing, balance, economy, projection and the artful stress on a seemingly-unimportant fact which leads to the unexpected climax. Mostly amateurs only remember the tag line and make a complete hash of the build-up needed to ensure the belly laugh at the end.

So – can you really tell a funny story? Most people think they can but only a minority have minds really equipped to do so. Frankly not everyone who boasts of possessing a sense of humour actually does so. If analysed they would discover their 'humour' was turned on like a tap; they laugh at comedians because they expect to do so. However, face them with some spontaneous situation such as a comic occurrence at a funeral, and they would remain merely appalled. The true humorist would react differently, at once seeing the funny side even if he or she does manage to hide their amusement. Humour is not confined to jokes or set patterns of entertainment but is a general outlook on life itself. True humorists are usually people slow to anger and quick to compassion.

Humour is a gift of course. Really excellent raconteurs, amateur or professional, who know exactly what to stress and what to omit, will often use dialects, if they have that knack, to colour their anecdotes. They fuse fun into their subject, adding information and illustrating points. They do not, in a speech, begin as do some inexperienced speakers: 'Have you heard the one about the Irishman who ...' Often, if the story is currently doing the rounds, someone in the audience will shout 'yes' ... or, even more demoralisingly, wait until the tag line is imminent – and then loudly finish the joke for the speaker! Nor, as we touched on in Chapter 3 under 'Timing' does the expert forget to insert important information in the build-up so that after the joke has fallen flat, he has to confess he forget to explain that the central character was a plumber. How professionals cringe when they hear a perfectly effective story completely wrecked by being told badly.

Never use the gimmick of twisting a fictional joke to make it sound 'fact' about a real person. Professionals often do this as seen on television award nights when one will relate a ludicrous story about another, usually on his sex life or financial meanness. This ploy is understood and accepted in showbusiness publicity but when amateurs try it the results can be disastrous, especially if the person they are trying to lampoon is a stranger to them. We recall one young man at a dinner telling a sexy story about the next speaker being in bed with his wife. The room suddenly went icy cold. The unfortunate victim of that contrived joke had only just attended his wife's funeral. Abject apologies had to be made and that speaker was never asked again.

The skill of public speaking is never more evident than in a speaker's use of humour. The wit and ingenuity they use to illustrate valid points gives them their reputation. They know exactly the *bon mot* for given situations and never offend. Because they are considerate they command respect.

The application of humour in public speaking is more likely to cause bad errors of judgement than any other facet. The best speakers use humour as apt observations on life. Lesser speakers are liable to confuse satire with ridicule, sometimes quite unwittingly, to show up ignorance, which might well have a systemic cause rather than be anybody's personal fault. Pointed and 'sick' jokes are inserted misguidedly – and when analysed finally show the innate weaknesses of the speaker's sense of humour.

A good exercise, when considering humour in public speaking, is to study any item you intend using under the 'personal puff' category. If an anecdote or joke is liable to show you up in a 'clever' light or make you sound self-satisfied, omit it – or readjust it to avoid any possible charges of self-aggrandisement. If humour is too one-sided – giving an impression that you *know* you are being witty – an audience will react by thinking you 'too clever by half'!

The best humorous speakers are those who use illustrative anecdotes *against* themselves. They make themselves appear victims of a situation rather than the skilful instigators of it. For example, the rustic who answers a learned question with a highly unexpected but profound reply; or the innocent child who caps an adult remark with a blissful, simple phrase, the logic of which leaves you gasping. Such anecdotes never fail to please audiences. And, by making himself the butt of his own subject, the speaker is enjoyed as a character, for he is proving he is fallible, human and as gullible as the next man. Describing how you have been caught out or made to look foolish is the safest form of humour any speaker can use.

Of course in commercial or political speaking, humour is not always a wise weapon. It might please those within your cause but will be treated with contempt by your opponents. In commerce people are very easily affronted – especially if you hit on a near truth! An innocent jibe can cause all sorts of ruffled tempers. So, if your job depends on it, watch the use of humour in any form when on your feet. The sly dig may become a graveyard of hopes!

Therefore it is with the social communities that you will be most likely to use humour to entertain within your subject. The desire to raise laughter must be compassionate so analyse very carefully any item you wish to include in your speeches. Will it possibly offend *anyone*? Racial or religious references are most certainly bound to upset someone in the body of the hall unless the references are discreet and congenial. No clergyman in your audience minds a witty crack at the church if it is apposite to your subject – but it must be basically kind.

The best exponents of speech humour are often lawyers and doctors, because their respective professions bring them into contact with life in the raw. They represent law and health and audiences will often accept quite barbed humour from them because they know they are in the hands of professionals. But they will not accept a layman copying the doctor's or lawyer's lines. In his mouth the same observations will die a death. Certain anecdotes are the prerogative of specialists within their field – a fact beginners often ignore, to their cost.

Rehearse your comedy aspects thoroughly as you would the rest of your speeech. Do not just put a heading on your cue card; 'Tell joke about the oyster' without bothering with the bridging link. Humour must be merged into the mainstream of the speech as a natural progression. Rehearse it diligently. Many otherwise good speakers fall flat when it comes to comedy. They feel it is compulsory or conventional to include a joke in any speech they make – but often it is the weakest part of it.

You will have to be ruthless with yourself when deciding on humour in your speeches. Can you truthfully handle it sufficiently well? Many of you will be blessed with wit, drollery or a sense of the ridiculous. But perhaps not all three. Humour is intricate, diversified. All comedians possess different styles and techniques and the best know better than to tackle branches of comedy beyond their scope. So, too, must the public speaker find his true niche, be it sophisticated or broad comedy, the debonair or the tattered clown – but never mix the two.

Certainly try and infuse humour, even lightly, wherever you can. A ripple of amusement in an otherwise serious discourse can do nothing but good so long as it is in context and promotes further understanding of the subject. The fact that the audience react to the humour spontaneously means that you have their full attention and your words are getting through to them.

With humour as with other types of speech material you can use a filing system as described in Chapter 4, listing anecdotes and stories under various headings. As we also discussed earlier many can be adapted to suit different occasions by adjustment and interchange of personnel and locale to please a majority of audiences.

We stress again that the real-life anecdote with its authenticity and substantiated characters is the most effective use of humour to enhance a point. The basis of truth is the vital ingredient which gives a speech authority. The fictional joke remains better material for the bar afterwards.

Remember, too, the old theatre adage handed down from comedian to comedian as they grew wiser ... 'if in doubt, leave it out'. . . .

8

Lectures and Specialised Talks

If you are an authority on a particular subject, you may well be able to give an interesting lecture or luncheon club talk. Most thinking people have a special interest – scientific, political, literary, sport – or indulge in community activities which deal in depth with social problems. Your specific job or any part-time pursuit could possibly furnish you with sufficient material to instruct others. Certainly such topics as cookery, dress-making, flower arrangement, gardening or interior design and many more allied topics have always found a ready market among women's clubs. However, not all our hobbies – or hobby horses – are of such general interest that people not similarly addicted will bother to come and hear us expound on them.

The luncheon club talk must be primarily educative. The women's societies, who are the mainstays of such speakers, want information as a priority. Entertainment, while it must be present, is the lesser consideration. They do not want jokes. They will certainly laugh if your anecdotes relate entirely to your subject – but humour is by no means a necessary ingredient.

Lectures on subjects with which the audience have no personal association have to be written most perceptively to avoid blinding them with science or being technically over their heads. To succeed with a talk of this kind you must endeavour to relate it in some way to the *milieu* of the audience. That is not to say you must confine *topics* within a certain environment. The wider the adventure the better the interest, but lecturers must remember in telling their story or describing an unusual procedure that the information must be phrased in a style compatible with the listeners' intelligence. This is not 'playing down' to them in a patronising way, but getting the message across to those who, while having no previous knowledge of it, nevertheless are very astute in other directions. As school teachers understand the difference between instructing a primary school and the sixth form, so lecturers have to consider their subject-presentation in similar ratios in adult standards of understanding.

Deciding whether or not you have an attractive subject for the lecture circuits needs very careful thought. Some themes that seem, at first, obvious choices are not always such cast-iron certainties. Burglaries, fire-prevention, health and safeguarding the home against intruders do not easily find a market among the after-lunch talk audiences. Vital though all such topics are, the subjects are for the class-room atmosphere, rather than after a good meal. There is an 'unpleasant', unentertaining ring to them. They are better left to police officers, firemen, general practitioners and the like to deliver on coldly instructional courses.

A 'local' expert might be the exception that proves this rule because he is known by the audience before he speaks. But that same address would not be so popular with strange audiences. A good example is that of insurance officials; usually the soundest of advisers on fire and theft prevention in the home, they are treated with suspicion by lecture organisers who may well feel that their club will be treated to a hard 'sell' for some specific insurance company. Speaking agencies naturally fight shy of any talk that may be construed as advertising propaganda. Perhaps the nearest they get to it is using stately home owners who lecture on their historic mansions which are also open to the public!

Sport, too, is a very limited field unless you have won at Wimbledon or have achieved other world status and can bring your gold medal to prove it. Even then, especially in women's club talks, the interest is more psychological than the need for practical demonstration of the games' skill. Achieving any form of stardom is fascinating to them, but they derive the biggest value from the effect of success on daily life and the changes in circumstances of the individual.

If you do possess expertise on a workable subject, analyse it carefully under both 'cultural' and 'practical application' in relation to prospective audiences. Certainly 'travel' lectures usually go well, but they have to be delivered entertainingly to keep the interest of people who have not been through your experience and are never likely to do so. Remote aspects should be presented with plenty of explanation, keeping the audience's own life-style in mind, if necessary drawing comparisons with that and the mystery world you are unveiling to them.

As in all forms of public speaking, the lecturer must give his or her audience a feeling of involvement. When drafting a talk or lecture keep 'culture' 'information' and 'entertainment' firmly in mind. Consider exactly what value the uninitiated will gain from it.

Audiences enjoy snippets of unusual information, especially about people – even though they may, in their future conversations, trot them out as their own! Some are avid for educative items which can improve their personal dialogue. It may be considered a vanity, but it is the age-old value of gossip. Only a minority of it is troublesome; the majority of information passed on is valuable and should not be allowed to die without further narration down the generations.

If you remain entirely outside or above an audience's orbit, they will be bored – and very cross indeed if they are paying you! They expect you to provide them with new thoughts for their money, they want to quote you, whether they actually acknowledge the source or pretend it is their own. You have to feed that desire, regard them as intelligent students on a new course of instruction – but with plenty of aptitude.

Never at your peril ridicule in your mind such audiences. If you do you will instinctively sound patronising. Lecturers in their time meet many big fish in small ponds and can be irritated by their apparent self-importance and their desire to be seen rubbing shoulders with VIPs. To you, it may seem petty, but such people are almost always the life-blood of communities. Their vanity is their value. They work hard for their prestige, are often perhaps intolerant of competition from outside – but, within their own district, provide a great many needs. It can be said their ultimate goal is local limelight, but they strive strenuously to provide it for themselves by engineering some extremely pleasant functions.

On their travels, of course, lecturers will meet those who exhibit seemingly outmoded and extraordinary prejudices. There was one ladies club committee who refused to engage Sir Alec Rose, the round-the-world yachtsman, because he used films – and they stated emphatically that they did not want to hear him sitting in the dark! No argument would alter that attitude, so all lecturers needing photographic support on screen had to stay away. But however pedantic you may consider such organisers, they call the tune when paying you to pipe.

Making a start

You have to prove yourself worthy of hire before you can get on the lecture or after-lunch circuits. Once you feel you have a genuine lecture on a broadly interesting topic, you must first find your own audiences. Offer your services to local church hall gatherings, schools, student groups, associations, old people's homes and community centres. Thus you will become practised in making adjustments to different types of audience and age-groups.

There is no easy beginning to this form of public speaking. You are in at the deep end from your first experimental lecture. If you are at university or polytechnic break the ice in front of your fellow students. As you know, they will be more critical than many audiences you will face in the future! That is all to the good. You need no humbug, no flattery. If you intend to be a professional, stiff criticism early on is the best way of achieving fluency.

A speaking agency will want their representative to hear you in action before enrolling you. The only lecturers they will take on before some form of audition are those already reputable on, say, radio or television. Such is the power of the media – although for certain audiences, the 'unknown' is so often the better speaker than the celebrity. Many a star has had his or her come-uppance when facing a ladies luncheon club because they have presumed too much on 'reputation' to carry them through. They have appeared all smiles but with basically very little to say, thinking their very presence is all that is required. Usually to their cost they discover that they have badly misjudged both the audience and their own 'fame'.

Naturally fame helps a speaker – he or she does have a head start on the unknown – but it *is* only a head. If a star is disappointing the let-down for the audience is the greater. An unknown who warms into a talk pleasantly and engagingly, who has something informative to say, soon compensates for that 'head' start. Once an audience is sitting enthralled, who cares about the speaker's background. That is why the lecture world so often makes its own 'stars' from men and women completely unknown outside it. Societies recommend to each other lecturers who have pleased them – and the really popular ones are given their own VIP status, a splendid state of affairs!

One recalls a young girl who, on delivering her first after-lunch talk, admitted it to the audience right away. 'I'm new to this,' she said, 'so if I go wrong, tell me. You know more about it than I do.' They warmed to her because they had, after all, listened to speakers every week for years. So, when asked back during a later season, she found she had become a sort of personal possession of that society. They had launched her career and were very proud of her indeed.

Once you have compiled and delivered a good talk a few times and feel the results justify your taking it up professionally, arrange that a speaking agency hears you. They are always on the look out for new speakers but they do, as we stress, need that degree of artistry that merits a fee. This means you must sustain rehearsal. You can use notes of course, but the delivery must be fluent and untrammelled. You have to work a lecture up to as near perfection as possible on local audiences before trying your luck on the professional circuits.

All such speakers, incidentally, lecture as an ancillary to their ordinary work. This may mean if you are in a regular job you may not be able to take time off to indulge in this pin-money exercise. You have to be free during the middle of the week and be prepared to travel sometimes considerable distances. A car is almost essential these days. Some veterans still travel by plane, train or coach, but this often involves extra cost for those booking them because they have to be met and time schedules strictly adhered to. An evening lecture would involve hotel expense overnight for example and most societies are on a very tight budget. One must remember these organisers are amateurs with other commitments in life, so meeting and returning speakers to stations and airports or finding them hotels is an added burden on their time besides causing additional expenses. Sometimes they feel a speaker with a high reputation is worth it but, in the main they prefer those who are self-contained, who arrive, do the job well and leave without extra cost or organisation. We discuss this aspect in more detail in the next chapter.

An apt title

You compile a lecture as you would a speech in extended form. You sort out the points you wish to make, put them in a correct order and obtain a balance between information and entertainment supporting it.

Then you must give it an absolutely crystal clear title. 'Over The Hills And Far Away' may sound cosy, but it does not tell the prospective audiences whether those hills are in Gloucester, California or New South Wales. The title should be 'A Study of the Cotswolds' or 'The Blue Mountains of Australia' so that, when the town hall posters go up or the secretary circulates his club membership with forthcoming events, those interested will know exactly what to expect. Do not try to give a talk a 'bookish' title. 'Theatre in the Late Nineteenth Century' is a far better title than 'The Days of Gas Footlights'; 'The Life of Franz Schubert' is more readily understood than 'The Unfinished Symphony'.

Literary or coy titles are the bane of agents. Organisers want complete clarity of content in pre-lecture publicity. The agent has to sell that title to them in the first place. Being arty-crafty will drive people away, but a good, down to earth, obvious title will give them the information they need. As one caustic agent told us : 'If your subject is jam-making in the Himalayas, say so!'

Presentation of talks

Your lecture subject is more important than your personality. That the two must be compatible is obvious but, as we stressed earlier, you are more likely to succeed as an 'unknown' who delivers an educative talk entertainingly than a 'star' who relies on material geared to reveal how amusing or clever he or she is. The audience want value for the ticket money. Some sceptics may call them 'culture vultures' but they will peck your bones clean if you die a death!

Again one must guard against vanity in this field. It is up to a speaker, in effect, to 'listen' to his audiences as well as talk to them, imbibe the atmosphere and not give any impression that he is doing them a favour. In a lecture, like a speech, you should include relevant anecdotes, especially early on, so that you can judge by the strength of the laughter just how attentive or receptive each audience is. As you become experienced you will assess audiences fairly accurately although, as we discuss more fully in Chapter 13, there is always a degree of unpredictability about them.

Audiences which appear to have something else on their minds when you talk to them are a challenge. Your job will be to raise them out of that early dullness and sway them into keen absorption of your words. So aim to make your lecture as fool-proof as possible, cutting out parts that do not seem to register, rephrasing here and there, lightening heavy passages and keeping your voice sounding enthusiastic. If you drone or stay in one key, not even the finest material in the world will avoid some boredom. An audience can sense if a speaker is languid and only going through the motions.

You must appear interested in your subject yourself. If you look and sound keen to impart your information, revealing an eagerness to share it with them, you will be a success.

Question time

At the end of a luncheon club talk and at longer evening lectures, the chairman will suggest that members of the audience might like to ask questions. If your subject is a popular topic you will get plenty. However, if it is remote, say, about the Amazon or Tibet, you will know that the lecture needs rewriting if they cannot rustle up a few questions because you will not have made it sufficiently compatible with their own lives. Explorers often find this out when a questioner asks how their marriage partner felt on being left at home for such a long while! Thus someone, without any other link with your subject, is trying to involve themselves in the only aspect they can think of – being left behind – which in itself is a double-edged psychological reaction! So that domestic query becomes relative to a journey into unknown Tibet!

However you have to answer without flippancy, even if you feel annoyed that he or she has not gathered a more out-going aspect from your talk. Whatever questions your lecture prompts, however illogical you may deem them, you have to reply politely and sincerely. Then go home and revise the lecture to include more comparisons with your audience's daily lives and the Tibetans. There are many facets which can be relative, food, clothing, transport, weather, housing, local government ... you just have to insert and stress the difference between home conditions and those in that faraway land. It is very simple ... 'In Tibet there is no central heating as we know it. ...' That sort of construction helps someone unlikely ever to visit the place to make some sort of parallel with his own world.

Conversely there will be questioners, who are already well-versed in your subject and will jolt you with some additional information which you have missed. Always accept it with enthusiasm, however riled you may feel inside! One hates being caught out, but if the omission is your own you cannot blame the questioner. Thank them courteously for the information and never try to busk your way out of it. If valid you can include it in your next lecture on that subject. It is wise never to set yourself up as the complete expert or even allow those announcing you to do so. Far safer to leave room for others to add to your information.

You have to be prepared for this give and take at question time. Above all never offend any questioner, however arrogant or pompous he may sound. You may not even see them clearly if they are away at the back of the hall, just hear a sneering voice and your mind, at once antagonistic, puts an unpleasant face to it. Often they appear abrupt because they are inwardly trembling at their own audacity to stand up at all.

Question time demands both tact and patience. You will doubtless have questioners who try to 'upstage' you, bent upon reflected glory or stealing some of your limelight. You still remain courteous in your reply, even though the question is transparently asked to draw attention to their own knowledge.

For example, if you have made a mere passing reference to the fact that to study tropical vegetation in Africa you travelled by plane, some aeronautical 'expert' might demand to know what sort of aircraft you used. Possibly you will have no idea of its name or design and know no more than it was small, light and took off from Nairobi! The questioner however is asking you this so that he can steal a bit of thunder by answering the query himself. You find this ploy often in lecturing. If you admit you do not know the details the floodgates are open for the questioner to show off his knowledge. You could have replied: 'If you knew all that beforehand why raise the question?' – but you don't. You thank him politely for the information and leave the audience to make their own assessment of its value. Mostly they will be on your side as they will doubtless have heard that egocentric many times before!

One way to overcome a persistent and obviously hostile questioner is to say that time is getting short but you would be happy to have a word with him afterwards as the topic he has raised would take rather a long time to answer. Be sure, of course, you *do* see him when the lecture is over so that at least he can have his pound of flesh – but in a quiet corner, preferably with a glass in your hand.

With domestic topics, the questions will flow fast, old adages quoted and additional remedies and hints added to those you have mentioned. However, if it is your experience that your subject is inclined to leave them stranded for ideas at question time, rewrite certain portions so that you insert, purposely, controversial points about which you can say: 'Perhaps, after I've finished, some of you may like to question me on these aspects.' Thus you set their minds into the correct channels – and, later, up they will pop to have their say.

If question time is greeted with an entirely mute response then you may have to invent a few questions of your own. So you would preface your question time introduction with 'Perhaps you are wondering how, in the course of this experience, I managed to ...' or ... 'perhaps you may be interested to know that, as a result of this expedition, my youngest daughter asked me ...' and so develop more mundane or off-the-beaten-track questions. Such little twists of dimension can often prompt questions which, even if only indirectly connected with the subject, will give questioners the chance they want to take the floor.

Question time does bring us back once again to being sure of your facts. Once you are challenged and proved wrong, the whole lecture loses credibility. If ever you have to take the count this way it is an unnerving experience. You can only apologise!

Very few questions are insincere, however, although there will also be occasions when someone, with sincere intent, asks something seemingly naive which may bring a scornful laugh from the audience. Never join in that derision. When dealing, say, with traffic problems, there is often an old lady who is worried that her cat might get run over. That is probably her sole concern with the problem you have discussed. She does not think of being run over herself, only the precious life of her pet. It is therefore a serious question from her point of view – and your answer must be considerate and compassionate.

There are, of course, 'propaganda' questions raised to put you on the spot, sometimes about local conditions about which you probably know nothing. A speaker on flower gardens was once asked by an indignant lady pet owner his views on the local council's ban on dogs running loose in the nearby park. It was a tricky question because the speaker was a stranger to the district. He could not evade the question, loaded though it was, nor yet take sides in an obviously controversial issue. By skilfully avoiding the town council's new ruling, he concentrated upon the effect of dogs on flowers and foliage – which *was* his subject – without offending the lady's beliefs or the opinions of the rest of the audience. By sticking rigidly to his brief no one could complain.

Often an innocent question will give you a new lead for your lecture, because it may prove that you have been hitherto understating an aspect which required more clarity. After a long speaking stint question time might seem arduous but it does have the advantage of keeping the actual material fresh by the occasional revision based upon what you learn from audiences. Certainly the personal contact you have with them at question time means they are personally involved in exchange of ideas. That is the one great difference between lectures and ordinary speech audiences. The public speaker does not often suffer contradiction save perhaps in the hearers' minds but the lecturer must be prepared to be answered back!

9

Stage Managing your Public Speaking

In speech-making and lecturing you are not only author and performer but also your own producer and stage manager. You have to put your show on the road even to being your own property master and wardrobe mistress. Fully enjoying public speaking depends so much on your peace of mind that not only is your speech satisfying to audiences but that the facilities for presenting it also give you a fair chance of success.

So let us take you through the administration which stems from your original invitation to speak at a function to saying goodbye when it's over. We will take as our main example an after-dinner speech as that needs a more comprehensive study than most other forms of engagement but, where necessary, we will differentiate to cover the needs of other functions.

If the invitation has been telephoned ask the organiser, if there is no eleventh hour pressure, to confirm all details in writing. A misheard instruction can cause havoc. 'Five' for 'nine', 'seven' for 'eleven' can mean the difference between a.m. and p.m. starting times or catching wrong trains. A name misunderstood might cause you to address someone wrongly in your speech, never a good beginning. So get your instructions on paper if time allows.

You need to know the following:

Name of the association you are addressing

Venue and type of function (luncheon, dinner, seminar, lecture, prize giving)

Time allotted for your speech

Any specific ingredients required in your material for it.

If you are proposing or replying to a toast you will need the names of the speakers who will be your opposite numbers in this context. If the engagement is professional, you must fix your fee, unless you are being booked by an agent, when he will obtain the contract.

You will also want to know whether the occasion demands formal dress (evening wear), or informal (which usually means dark lounge suits for men – not exposed hairy chests – and afternoon-style dresses for women). There may be no set dress format for some occasions but you do not want to be either too formal or too casual in relation to the rest of the guests. Appearance does matter and audiences can give you a frosty reception if they feel you have misjudged the occasion. If uncertain it is better to be too soberly dressed than shabby and unkempt!

You may also need to know in advance the name of the chairman of the occasion, names of other speakers and guests as you might want to refer to them in your speech. Any anecdote about a fellow guest makes for good team work between speakers and adds greatly to the enjoyment.

We have dealt with the effect of driving and speaking in Chapter 2 but there are other practical pointers to do with transport. If you are using your own car you will naturally check petrol, oil and tyres, so that the vehicle does not let you down on the journey. Punctuality on dates is essential, not only for your peace of mind but of those organising the occasion. Breakdowns, punctures, lack of petrol or traffic snarl-ups may be unavoidable in certain circumstances but if you have started off in good time, you can allow yourself leeway to make phone calls to advise those expecting you not to panic!

It is surprising how many experienced speakers are tardy in preparing themselves for the job and so give themselves unnecessary headaches when fulfilling engagements. Unpreparedness usually denotes laziness and doubles not only the speaker's anxieties but also those of the organisers as well.

If it is unfamiliar to you, check your road route with the organisers beforehand. Make a note of estimated time of arrival and obtain directions on parking facilities. This is vital. Many speakers turn up late full of apologies because they have been roving round a strange town looking for parking space, usually ending up a considerable distance from the venue. So arrange that the organisers make parking space available immediately adjacent to the hall or hotel at which you are speaking.

If you travel by public transport you should be met at the station or airport by a representative to take you personally to the venue. If no one can do this, then check that taxis are available, or, if within only a short walking distance, the exact map of the route. Some of these points will not always occur to organisers. They are so familiar with their own localities that they are liable to take it for granted that you, too, will know your way round.

Carry with you plenty of small change. This may be needed for emergency telephone calls, tips, refreshments, and use of public toilets en route. Purchase of a local newspaper on arrival is always a good investment as you may well hit upon a local community topic to write into your speech. This always impresses audiences and shows that you have taken trouble on their behalf.

Always bring tissues with you. These can act as substitute towels, shoe and spectacle cleaners, handkerchiefs, napkins, wiping the train's dirty windows for a view of the scenery, cleaning buffet car cutlery and a host of other little jobs which make for hygiene and travelling comfort.

Take your notebook with you on every journey. Ideas always occur en route to speaking dates. Your mind is attuned to the occasion and you often dream up last-minute improvements. You can, of course, also study your cue card en route on public transport if you have not yet fully 'broken in' the speech.

If you are being met by strangers, describe yourself frankly in a letter to the organisers beforehand so that, even in a large busy station depot or airport, they will know whom they are looking for. To be instantly recognisable it is a good plan to describe the overcoat, suit, hat and even the brief case you may be carrying. Be candid with the description ... I am short ... tall ... stout ... thin ... wear spectacles ... have beard or moustache ... with ladies the coat or dress, perhaps hair colouring.

The best plan is to arrange that you will stand stock still

beyond the last exit barrier through which you have to pass after leaving the plane, train or coach. Knowing that you will be static the representative can come and find *you*. It all saves valuable time especially at luncheon talks when hours are limited.

Sometimes, although it is far from satisfactory, organisers will meet you with a car but, owing to parking difficulties, they suggest you find them by seeking a make of car, colour, and a registration number. Be sure you have that number in your notebook.

All these pointers sound simple and, in some cases, obvious but it is amazing how often one vital link is overlooked, especially when arrangements are rushed as in the event of a speaker falling ill and a deputy being booked perhaps only the day before. He or she receives only garbled instructions, the result of consternation among the organisers. So, if you are ever that deputy, insist you have all the details absolutely watertight.

Make sure your watch is wound and is correct. 'My watch stopped' is a feeble-sounding excuse – but it seems to happen a lot on the speaking circuits.

Should you need manual assistance to get lecture equipment from your car on to the platform, arrange that with the organisers beforehand. Do not spring on them a delicate and tricky task without prior warning. If unprepared, all they will be able to call upon will be possibly willing but inexpert handlers. If breakages do occur you will only have yourself to blame if no notice has been given.

On arrival check with the secretary or chairman that the running order of events is as programmed and that there have been no last-minute changes. Sometimes those in charge forget that a speaker has been replaced by another and you may find yourself replying to a toast by naming the wrong person. So, as soon as you feel settled, check that your briefing is correct or make a note of any alterations affecting you. This attention to detail is all part of a good public speaking training. The speaker will not only earn a reputation for being reliable but also for keeping organisers on their toes ... better that than letting them tread on yours by inept, slapdash administration.

You may well feel that all this makes you a bit busy before you actually stand up and speak. But, in the early days, filling time this way is a great antidote to nerves. You have things to think about beyond the actual speech; you cannot dwell on that until you are sure all the arrangements are in order and personnel there as planned.

Anxieties often arise in new speakers' minds by lack of attention such as a taciturn neighbour at a dinner who will only converse with his friend on his left and leaves the stranger-speaker completely alone during the meal. This isolation can have a devastating effect on new speakers, and organisers should be aware of it. The passing time should be filled with conversation and integration with other guests.

People have different metabolisms and some, who are the most brilliant speakers, are nervous almost to stage-fright proportions every time they make a speech and will be for all their lives. Others, the mainstream, find experience gradually decreases those worries – but even the best speakers still suffer gnawing anxieties however many hundreds of speeches they have made. They want to do well and are taking nothing for granted. And if nerves do play a part in your speaking, then stage managing yourself before the event will keep you occupied and leave no time to cross bridges you may never reach, a common anxiety among speakers.

Allow yourself at least an hour to settle in before a function starts. You may well have to change into evening wear. If it is a lunch or dinner you will have plenty of time before you speak so you have the opportunity to fill it by checking arrangements. It is a form of unwinding some of us need – like taking that brisk walk which we mentioned in Chapter 2. So ensure you arrive early for a speaking date. Going straight on to the platform after a long harassing journey is not recommended as a good way of ensuring success!

Take time out to check where toilet and cloakroom facilities are in relation to the hall in which you are to speak. Beyond the obvious reason, that cold water wash with a dab on the back of the neck and temples can refresh you as well as dispel fatigue. Naturally if there is a drinks session prior to the meal or your speech, allow yourself only one to be sociable. Never drink over your limit if you are tired, otherwise you may create an over-confident tongue which a weary brain cannot correctly supply.

If time is available – and you should try and make it so – slip away and inspect the room, platform or stage upon which you will be speaking. Study your position in relation to the audience. At a dinner are they square on you or is the room L or T-shaped which means the majority of the audience are left and right of you rather than directly ahead of you? If the latter is the case, you will know that you will have to use plenty of head turns to encompass those on the peripheries of the room without losing contact with the microphone.

Perhaps the room for a dinner might be divided into a top table with others set in parties of eight or twelve, dotted about the floor in separate units. We know, from experience, that dinners so planned are the most difficult of all such speaking venues. If you see such a table plan be prepared to work harder than you might have to if everyone is seated at long sprigs branching from the top table, undivided from the rest of the room.

These individual tables for a mere handful of guests create little worlds of their own, with their own comedians and self-appointed leaders. Being an oasis for a few causes some extrovert member to take over the table and become its unofficial spokesman. If he happens to think himself a funny man, he has his own little captive audience.

Psychologically these isolated table units create rival factions within the audience as a whole. If seated all together they will blend but, spaced as groups, they become tightly-knit and engender different moods from those of their neighbours. Thus you are liable to get alternate pockets of attentive and inattentive people, some keen to listen, others desiring to make some sort of vocal contribution to your speech themselves. This happens almost always at social dinners but can be most irritating when the well-wined spoil the fun for others.

Separate tables create a 'them' and 'us' situation with the

top table more visibly 'select'. You have to be on best form when facing such a room. Head movement will have to be used a great deal to encompass all these tables. It is no good fixing your eyes on the wall opposite and never wavering from it. This will only make these groups feel more isolated than ever. Your job is to try and mould these small 'communities' into one cohesive audience.

Knowledge of these strange quirks in public speaking are all part of experience and you will cope but organisers themselves should consider this aspect very closely when running functions involving such a table plan. If facilities are such that separate tables must be used, the groups should be of never less than twenty or thirty so that there is a good nucleus of support for good behaviour in each unit. Even better to appoint a reliable 'chairman' from the committee to control each table.

However it is significant that ladies lunch clubs often use this seating system through force of circumstances in their venues, but never create this problem for speakers. Why is it always the men who employ these 'take over' tactics? All-women audiences are sometimes a little less flexible but they are certainly far more chivalrous!

Microphones

Before the function try if you can to test the microphone or, at best, see that someone else does it. Often when several speakers are involved, by the time the microphone reaches you it is either forehead high or down below your chest. If there is no steward at your elbow, you may well have to adjust it yourself. So familiarise yourself with the process, see which nut allows you to loosen the stem and that it slides up or down easily. Then you will not waste valuable time when on your feet, struggling with a strange microphone in full view of the audience. It does not help nerves in early speaking to have such unexpected problems just before you start.

If you can test the microphone yourself, so much the better. You can check balance and ensure you are speaking the correct distance away from it. It may not be possible to achieve this check if guests are already assembling in the room but, if you can get there early enough, you can get a valuable 'feel' not only of the microphone and your position as a speaker but of the room itself, its depth, width and lighting. Just explain to the head waiter (or whoever else is in charge) and he should give you every assistance.

Never be afraid to carry out these checks. Organisers are apt to take a lot for granted, especially when the VIPs have arrived and the drinks are flowing prior to the meal. Because there was not a hitch at their last function they may presume all arrangements are in the same right order. But plugs can be accidentally kicked out by passing waitresses. Bad microphones may wheeze and crackle and the evening be held up while amateur electricians risk their lives to repair them with dessert forks – in the middle of your speech!

The introduction of you as a speaker

Someone will announce you as the next speaker. If you are a stranger to the audience, check beforehand with whoever will be in charge, that he has his facts about you completely correct. If he has only received scant information he will be glad of a prompt from you on your background.

If you want any special aspect of your career stressed then tell them. This is not vanity; just plain commonsense. It may well be that your hobby rather than your job is the prime reason for you speaking that night. So that must be made clear to the audience. In our own cases, we, the authors, are both professional entertainers and writers. In our speaking stints we usually appear as only representing one of our two jobs. So whoever announces us is asked to underline whichever aspect covers our speech. Thus, it will be with you. Most people today have several facets any one of which can prompt a public speech ... so if a lawyer is going to talk on sport, his expertise on the latter is the more important information for the audience. So often speakers, poorly announced with all the wrong reasons being given for their presence, have to spend valuable time adjusting the data.

Toastmasters in particular are always glad of additional information from a speaker with which to embellish their announcements. A good introduction saves you valuable speaking time. Before you begin your talk, the audience are absolutely clear in their minds of your intentions, no one has to back-track or amend anything and the event flows on smoothly.

Checking that the announcement you will receive is both correct and relevant is particularly valid in lecturing. It is more important that the audience hear proof of your expertise than hear a general biography which pays no heed to your exact qualifications to be there.

Use of intervals at meal functions

When appearing as a speaker in the more protracted occasions of luncheons and dinners, you will find a personal routine invaluable. There is always an interval between coffee and the announcement of the first speech. As one of the speakers, it is a good tip to excuse yourself as soon as possible after the last course so that you can avoid a crowded washroom when the audience itself finally files out to use it. If you wait until the interval is actually announced you can find yourself on the end of a long queue, especially if the accommodation is limited as in small hotels or church halls. This means only a rushed hand rinse, soggy towels and a limited view of a small mirror to tidy hair or adjust tie, with virtually no chance of rinsing out the mouth or indulging in that useful cold dab on the nape of the neck.

So slip away earlier (even if it means missing the sweet course) so that you can be sure of more or less complete freedom of the washroom. However always inform someone in authority – the secretary, chairman or toastmaster – of your intention; otherwise it could happen that you are announced before you are back in the room!

If a clothes brush is available, use it to disperse ash, crumbs, even dandruff or falling hair. It is surprising how dark clothing will pick up flotsam in the smartest of venues.

Use your tissues to dab water on the nape of the neck and

temples especially if the atmosphere in the dining room has been warm. Then give your nose a good blow to clear the sinuses as that interval is also a call for smoking in the audience. By leaving early you can avoid the first cigarette and cigar flare up but you will still have to speak through it.

If possible rinse your mouth out to free it from food particles. Nothing is worse than speaking with a strand of meat firmly wedged between molars. If your teeth are liable to trap food, carry a toothpick. Should you wear dentures ensure you have a safe fixative. Today there is little excuse for dentures slipping. However as many professional speakers know, the sudden change from their own teeth to dentures needs a period of adjustment and they take time out from the circuits to rehearse with the new set. So pay attention to dentures before speaking for you must feel secure. Getting that washroom to yourself can be an especial boon in this connection.

Your spectacles should be cleaned whether you need them only for notes or if you wear them permanently. An audience is a mass of humanity generating heat and glasses are apt to cloud over. Again those tissues in the handbag or pocket can be a great asset if you need that quick wipe over the lenses within the room itself.

When you feel presentable in appearance and calm in mind you can stroll back to your seat just as the main body is setting off *en masse* to tidy up – but in far more cramped conditions. Using the interval in this manner ensures that you have at least a quarter of an hour at the table on your own to study your notes and make any adjustments based on your assessment of the audience after sitting through the meal among them. If you have had rather talkative neighbours either side of you during the dinner – always a good thing on such occasions – you now have time to concentrate without interruption.

This time alone at the table enables you to cater for any late changes in the programme which might affect your speech and is generally a settling-in period. Then as the other guests begin to filter back you can sit back and study them, getting some idea of their mood and receptiveness. Good organisers should make sure that you, as a speaker, have preferential treatment at such intervals but it is sometimes difficult for them, especially if they have several guests to entertain or a VIP who commands all their attention. If this is the case you are better off stage-managing yourself to make sure you freshen up and relax prior to your speaking stint.

You must now, in the role of your own 'producer', ensure that you do not overrun the time allotted you. Should you be speaking in support of a celebrity whom the audience has come primarily to hear, then remain the supporting player. Certainly give of your best but do not poach on his or her time. Set this example and, when you yourself become the star attraction perhaps those supporting you will keep the rules as well.

During the actual meal avoid eating and drinking too much. The wine waiter may be lavish, the waitress may suggest second helpings as you are a top table guest, but if you feel distended when you rise to speak, indigestion can strike. Your breathing becomes laboured, which is no help in projecting your voice. However experienced a speaker might feel himself to be, a full stomach is a handicap to his personal enjoyment in delivering his speech – and can be very injurious to health generally. Also an inadvertent hiccup into the microphone is worse than all the 'ums' and 'ers'.

There are occasions where you might be staying overnight in the same hotel at which you are speaking. This is a great advantage for, during that interval, you may well be able to slip up to your bedroom for freshening up. Then you can actually brush your teeth – never forget a toothbrush – which is a real godsend before returning to a heavily atmosphered room. Again be sure you inform an official where you are going.

Dress

Clothes must feel easy about you. The throat should naturally be unrestricted. Young men in borrowed evening dress often find the shirt a size too small. As the room heat increases, bow ties begin to bulge. This makes an extra and unnecessary hazard to good speaking. When that bow is knotted, you should be able to insert two fingers quite comfortably between collar and throat so that you have full breathing space. When you stand up and take that good lungful of air it will have full effect. Deep breathing at this stage, just before you begin communicating with the audience, has a steadying effect on stomach nerves. Four deep breaths as you are being announced works wonders.

Ladies are rarely encumbered by dress but that neat necklet so easy to clasp on in a cool bedroom could well tighten up in a hot dining room if the neck swells even slightly. Perversely, if too loose, it could work its way round the neck during your speech so that the centre piece ends under your ear. It is better to leave the throat bare of ornament unless a high-necked dress is worn but ensure that, like the man's collar, it is wide enough for complete comfort. Necklaces are a good adornment for ladies, provided you do not twiddle or fidget with them during your talk, which happens sometimes during the learning days.

Ladies have to be very careful of jewellery. If it flashes when caught in the light it can be most disconcerting to audiences even though the speaker could not have foreseen such a hazard when she dressed. Flickering gems can be an awful nuisance to people looking at you. If you are lecturing, for example, it is wise to leave such adornments, especially long-swinging pendant ear-rings, in their cases. You cannot anticipate lighting problems, so play safe. Dining halls, too, are inclined to have mirrored walls which further reflect glitter. And there is, too, a personal aspect, that of looking too opulent for the audience's taste. It is pointless adding 'envy' to their reaction!

Bangles and bracelets can be troublesome if, when you gesture, they clink up and down your arm. Full, long, flowing sleeves have been known to sweep a glass of wine into the chairman's lap. Gestures should not be 'sweeping' anyway but, if you are prone to use them, then have your sleeves tailored. Through not rehearsing in the outfit she intended to wear at a function a lady once had trouble reading notes between the microphone and her full-fronted, frilled blouse which completely obscured her hands unless they were held right up to her face.

A slim line is recommended to all ladies. Remember that, especially at meal functions, you are also sitting for an hour or two at least, so very full skirts can become uncomfortable in a narrow chair. At some less formal events you may well appear in a trouser suit.

A change of shoes is often a good idea if you have travelled a long way and can still feel the brake pedal or hard paving stones. Many a male speaker slips on a pair of inconspicuous black house shoes at occasions when he knows his feet will be covered from the audience by a table cloth. If you can avoid it, never make a speech wearing brand new shoes. Again the heat of the room can cause foot expansion, a nagging tightness on toe, heel and instep, which, when standing, is most disconcerting to clear thought. People are apt to forget feet in public speaking but, if you have a lecture or speech of over half an hour, you may hobble back to your seat if your footwear has been too tight.

As we mentioned in Chapter 3, under that same table cloth ladies can slip off their shoes ... but it may be a struggle to replace them when the feet have expanded and cause a lot of stooping and gasping! As one famous lady speaker once admitted: 'After speaking at dinners I became very adept at levering my shoes back on a with fork handle. During the meal I used to hide one under the menu to avoid waiters clearing it away. But one night the chairman thought I was stealing the cutlery – so now I carry a small shoe horn in my handbag. ...'

This is a typical example of how public speakers improvise their own routines as they go from engagement to engagement. You will find you too will invent many do-it-yourself aids to your speech-making. Some hints we have listed here you may or may not want to use but you will, nevertheless, devise other 'insurances' for yourself. Anything you can stage-manage for your own peace of mind as a public speaker will make the end product the better for it.

Visual aids in lectures

Besides slide or film projectors there may be other visual aids some lecturers or instructors need. Maps, models, plans, even specimens of some kind, are often required, especially for purely educational or commercial talks. Schemes and projects need to be illustrated so, before you step on to the rostrum, inspect the venue and make sure that all such visual aids are visible to *all* your audience. In business ventures when the audience may be less than a dozen, you can talk from behind a table and have your exhibits on it for all to see. They are also within easy reach so you can, if necessary, pick them up while speaking.

At a larger venue, small exhibits are not advised. The front rows might be able to see a rare fossil as you hold it up but those at the back will be well beyond sight range and feel somewhat cheated. Always ensure that everybody has a fair chance of seeing any exhibits you may wish to discuss. If you have to use very small items, we suggest you discuss them in the lecture but put them on view *after* your talk so that those interested can file round, armed with the information you have already given them.

Certainly if you are using film or slide projection, rehearse with the operator if he is a stranger to you. Make sure he knows your cues. If verbal that he has a script to follow, if by a clicker from the lecturer's hand, that he can hear it plainly! These suggestions may seem obvious to the most naive beginner but because they are so fundamental, they are often forgotten.

People running functions are apt to get their priorities misaligned. In rushing to receive the lord mayor and handing out drinks in the reception room, nobody has checked the lecture hall light fuses. So, as the proceedings get under way, the place is suddenly plunged in darkness. It should not happen if a function is properly run. Alas, human nature being what it is, too often those in charge desire, above all, to rub shoulders with the VIPs while ticket-holders, perhaps quarrelling over duplicated seat tickets, are left to work it out for themselves.

If you happen to be the speaker on such occasions, through no fault of your own, you may get off to a bad start. The poor preliminary arrangements reflect back on you; a disgruntled audience, suffering fused lights, confusion in seating, broken film or slides upside down, will be very hard for you to lift up from sullen discontent.

Pianos

Some lecturers and after-lunch speakers are musicians and will need a piano. If you should be in this select group, insist the piano is tuned on the day of your appearance. Write or telephone the secretary of the society and really insist on this necessary service. Non-musical people are inclined to think any piano will do but if your talk is on a serious plane, the keyboard illustrations must be absolutely in tune otherwise you might as well cancel the date.

When you arrive check the piano for both tone and position. The audience must see you while you play so get assistance to move it to the angle best suited to the seating plan.

Checking venues for lectures

Walk round that hall, test the microphone and see how far back your audience will reach so that you can be sure that those at the rear can both see and hear. Some halls are very primitive and you will need to improvise perhaps, but, if you have arrived late, you will have no chance to rectify deficiencies at all. Nothing is worse than having to adjust to adverse conditions *during* your actual talk. Much better to be an hour early and smooth out any trouble spots which may not only affect the audience's pleasure in your talk, but also your enjoyment in delivering it.

If an agent has booked you, he should have given you plenty of information as should the organisation's secretary if you have been engaged direct. If you are working on a stage or rostrum check some time before the event if there will be a table or lectern available. Certainly when using notes on such a platform a lectern is invaluable as it leaves the hands free, is usually adjustable to the exact height and some have a hooded strip-light which is a boon in a darkened hall.

See that you have a carafe of water and a glass – and make no bones about taking a sip during your lecture if your mouth dries. No need to make funny remarks about it not being gin, either. Moistening the mouth is an accepted pause in any speaker's time on his feet.

List your needs for the organisers and make sure, when you get there, they are at your disposal. And the best way to ensure this is to arrive early and check all facilities for yourself including knowing where the toilet is in relation to your stage.

Lighting

Speaking in artificially-lit halls needs close attention. Often a speaker hurries on, late, to an unfamiliar platform only to find when he rises that his notes are in deep shadow. This means embarrassing delays while he changes position of lectern or table. The organisers may have thought that one single light bulb would be sufficient for the lecturer's requirements, but **they** had not studied its position. They will however respect your precision if you make changes before the audience troop in, but if you panic them when once the seats are filled, the result will only be makeshift and not improved by frayed tempers.

A shadow over your notes is bad enough but a constant shadow over your face is exasperating to the audience. If you find yourself on a reasonably equipped stage with front lighting – or even a spotlight – use it if it helps.

Sometimes in the after-dinner world spotlights are used on speakers, but these can be blinding if they have been set too low, as they often are, and shine right into the eyes. Occasionally, too, they are in the eyeline of members of the audience which soon brings angry complaints. Often a venue, usually a hotel, will improvise on their lighting equipment, using it for discos, dances, cabaret and after-dinner speakers. Rarely, if ever, does it suit everyone. While adequate in the ballroom, it is usually too strong – and far too near – for speeches, dazzling both speakers and audiences.

However, good lighting does add to the atmosphere of an occasion. An audience reacts favourably if all things are bright and clear. The single, naked, low wattage bulb above a speaker's head can have the depressing effect of gloom and penny-pinching. Organisers should, once again, be aware of this, but stage manage it yourself if you are not fully satisfied. Go to the back of the hall and as you test your microphone, so try out your lighting and make the best of what the hall has to offer. Do not be afraid to speak out against second rate facilities if you feel you can improve them. You want to feel on your best form to please the audience – and conscientious organisers will realise this.

After the function

If you have a train to catch and someone is giving you a lift to the station be sure you are ready to leave on time and do not be tempted by an extra gin. Missing trains means that you have been carried away by the hospitality afforded you after your speech and have not known when to say goodbye. It is a common fault but one to be avoided. The organisers, especially at luncheons, have to return to their normal routines with children to be met from school or offices to attend. If you hang about chatting, which happens when you have been particularly successful, those in charge may have to drop a few rather bald hints.

Never give organisers any chance to criticise your conduct. Speaking agents have heard the complaint often; 'Oh, yes, he was a fine speaker – but damned hard to get out of the bar afterwards'. If organisers make errors that is their look-out but you, as their guest, must be infallible, especially when keeping to a schedule.

That goes, too, for staying overnight in a hotel. Certainly do not run up a drinks bill in the bar and leave the organisers to pay for it. Sadly this often happens with celebrity speakers. They purposely take advantage of free drinks into the small hours and probably wreck the treasurer's budget for the occasion. When that happens the grapevine reacts against such persons for future engagements. The hosts have been quite happy to pay his fares or petrol, hotel meals and the bedroom, right up to morning tea – but not those personal expenses which are beyond the normal tacit agreement.

Another ploy with unscrupulous speakers is to turn up at dinners with a friend, demanding that he or she must sit beside him and have a free meal. That again upsets budgets, completely disrupts table planning and is thoroughly unethical. It is not uncommon for an invitation to include the speaker's wife or husband as an additional guest of the host society – but if they have not extended that hospitality do not presume upon it. If you bring along uninvited guests without first checking by telephone that it is possible and giving a very comprehensive reason why, you are never likely to be invited again yourself.

You may be given private hospitality in the home of a host society member. The situation arises when clubs have to economise on expensive hotels for their speakers and so officials take turns to play host to their guests overnight. Actually this is not always satisfactory especially if the speakers do not see their room until after the function. They can wander strange corridors at dead of night looking for the bathroom or, being over six feet tall, find themselves in a very short bed, but one can understand the thinking behind this form of hospitality. To save their club money your personal hosts are bearing the brunt of supplying you with a roof, bed linen which gives them laundry costs, and a breakfast with possibly a lift in their car to the station. The householders giving you such shelter probably have no idea before you arrive what size you are, whether or not you are a vegetarian, or are allergic to cats. Inwardly they are very nervous themselves, fearful of upsetting you, but they do their best.

You, for your part, have not the same facilities and service offered by a hotel but you must try and fit in with the host's domestic routine. It is likely, too, that they will invite their neighbours in to meet you after the function ... and expect you to tell your funny stories all over again for their benefit! There is a lot of one-upmanship in private hospitality – but that is not our business!

However, when you leave make sure you have their name and address and drop them a note of appreciation. Never take such hospitality as part of ordinary over-all organisation. Acknowledge it personally. On the speaking rounds you need all the friends you can get!

On the train home study the cue cards again and see if there is any room for improvement in the light of that last speech. You might well have inserted something useful during it so mark it in for future reference.

During an over-night stay check your cards before switching off the bedside light while your memory is still fresh. If you wait until you get home, tired and ready for bed, you may well forget any valuable question asked at your lecture or better formulae for presenting certain aspects of a speech which occurred to you when on your feet. It may be just one word you used that improved the speech – so jot it down before weariness blunts your recollection.

Fees

Once your lecture or talk becomes so popular as to bring you into professional status, you will have to return your fees against tax. Your agent will do so, so you cannot consider such payments as mere perquisites and keep them secret from the tax man! The societies at which you speak will also make tax returns against your engagement fee so it may be as well, if public speaking becomes a large part of your income, to use an accountant. There are certain expenses allowed for this work: he will know the ropes and how to apply for them.

Of course there have been speakers who have dodged this aspect of their income but always they are found out simply because their name has been on a menu or a report of their speech has appeared in a local paper. For tax purposes public speaking may also be considered part of promotion either of your business or artistic career, enhancing your reputation. For example, authors find it helps book sales. By its very nature the lecture or 'talk' is bound to be a subtle form of self-advertising which, in some walks of life, must improve financial prospects although not for all. Thus you are advised to use an expert to handle these aspects of a speaking career and obtain legitimate deductions.

If you work through an agent you will also show on your tax returns his commission deducted from your speaking fees. He will of course also guide you on the financial side of public speaking, even negotiating higher fees for your services as your popularity grows!

10

Television and Radio

Every passing day several thousands more people in ordinary walks of life find themselves facing television cameras. For some, that appearance may be the last but for a minority it will herald the start of a new chapter in their lives.

Closed-circuit television is now used by many large firms, linking New York with Zurich, London with Paris, Berlin with Sydney which saves the delegates having to travel long distances merely to sit round one council table. Time has become so pressing a commodity that these once seemingly innovatory ideas are now common practice. Whatever your role in life is now, it is fairly certain you will have to face cameras in the future so now is the time to adjust yourself to that prospect.

Beyond the closed circuits of commerce your most likely initiation on public television screens will be in interview form. Because you are an expert, a specialist or an important member of some planning team you may be singled out to give your views on a topical subject. It might be bitterly controversial, inciting the interviewer, to 'attack' to find loopholes in your argument or merely a placid explanation of an idea or system upon which he could be congratulatory. The latter situation will allow you time to think but the former will require you to be absolutely on the alert.

An already experienced public speaker starts with a great advantage for he or she is used to self-control. Television is a testing medium, the most exposing of all. It can be a vote loser for the nervous, as it will win support for the confident – and to the brash sometimes be a disaster. Quick thinking is demanded in interviews if the clock is not to beat you.

When possible, television stations prefer pre-filmed interviews so that tedious passages can be edited, mistakes erased and long pauses for thought pruned. The subjects who give the editors least trouble are the ones who will be asked back. So, when you face the cameras you must endeavour to give a competent performance, especially if it affects your job or a personal crusade.

The toughest example of television hazards is the street interview. Passers-by have a microphone stuck under their chins and a hand-held camera stares blackly into their face. The interviewer barks a question. It may be just a flippant, joke-type programme or a serious subject, as at election times, but for either you have to rely upon spontaneous reaction to answer. If you are already versed in public speaking you will, almost certainly, acquit yourself well.

Those in charge of news and magazine-type programmes can be quite ruthless. However charming they are to you personally their true intent is solely for their programme – and their job. They are not interested in any side effects a participant brings upon himself by a stupid observation on television. Often these programmes thrive on errors and those who make them become figures of fun both to the general public and worse, to those who know them personally. 'Did you see old Jones on the box last night? Made a right fool of himself....'

We stress this relatively small aspect of television because it illustrates exactly what the medium is all about. It can be magic for the disciplined speaker or misery for the unwary. A whole career can go down the drain through a lapse of concentration. If you can survive one of these interviews, you are ideal for the medium.

Where laymen inevitably go wrong is in forgetting the value of time. While they are busy preparing their thoughts, they are eroding valuable seconds which probably means their 'big' moment ends on the cutting room floor. TV programmes are planned to the split second. It may seem rough justice if you have a complicated argument to expound, but the rules must be obeyed. Brevity is the hall-mark of a good television speaker.

We often see on television a frustrated subject trying to rush an argument through only to be cut off half-way because, he is told soothingly, 'time has run out'. Yet if we could re-run that interview he or she began it by saying: 'Before I answer that, I would like to say. . . .' They have come to that studio with some preconceived ideas which may only have an indirect bearing on the theme, but are determined to voice it whatever the interviewer asks. So time runs out and the subject is left in limbo, having neither satisfied the viewing public nor the purpose of the programme.

Then there are those who use commercial jargon which they feel sounds 'educated' and so waste air time with phrases like 'at this moment in time' when 'now' or 'today' would save precious seconds, all of which can add up to a considerable period in an interview. Another is 'I, personally, am of the opinion that. . . .' 'I believe' covers the ground much faster. In the end an interview taking six minutes could have been pared down to three – and the additional time used really advantageously.

You are usually given time to settle in a studio interview. The commentator will give a few biographical details about you before he leads into the first question. Please do not preface your reply with 'Well, er. . . .' Millions of 'wells' are said on the air daily. And seconds tick by each time! School yourself to avoid these hesitancies.

Of course some interviewees without public speaking experience cannot avoid unnecessary verbiage . . . the housewife who ends every sentence with 'you know'. Another favourite is, 'so I said to her, I said . . .' or that strange sub-conscious cry for reassurance we mentioned earlier, 'I had to do the shopping, *didn't I?*' The amateur must be readily forgiven for such idiosyncratic dialogue, yet it is strange that they use more words per subject than ever it merits. With a limited vocabulary, however garrulous they are, they employ much repetition. So when their views are sought on the air, time almost inevitably runs out before the interviewer can extract something really valid from the chatter. If he has, it is because he has to put words into their mouths.

Television interviewers play a tactical game at which any good public speaker can also become proficient. When questioned he should not use up time with preludes and side-issues but, within his answers, embody the new dimensions of thought he needs to steer the argument into his channel ... which may not be the same as the interviewer's line of approach! So, under a form of 'prosecution', the 'defendant' needs fluency of thought and a needle-sharp awareness of the clock. He may even *stall* for time! And he will have to be on the *qui vive* for the 'trick' question, seemingly innocent, but set to trap him into an admission or contradiction which defeats his case.

We have all heard this type of approach:

Interviewer: 'You want the general public to support this strike?'

Subject: 'Of course ... we must draw attention to our demands ...'

Interviewer: 'But all you have done is *antagonise* the public. ...'

So, by a juxtaposition of priorities, the interviewer harps on *public* reaction while the subject tries vainly to voice the *internal* facts and *roots* of the dispute. In this case the interviewer is invoking the age-old anomaly of freedom which is never resolved, that of a man's right to withhold his labour when, by so doing, he deprives others of the liberty to follow *their* employment. This is an example of the 'over-simplification ploy', the widening of the spectrum just when the subject under fire wants it kept within its own four walls.

People who go on television to air a grievance are apt to forget that the interviewer will seek all he can to involve the viewing public in the dispute – and be on their side. He has to be; that is his job. So if ever it is your lot to be a protagonist in such circumstances, go to the studio prepared to involve the viewers, not merely just the two interested parties in conflict. As, mostly, such problems concern money you will have to be very astute to cope with apparently justified moral approaches on behalf of people who are not going to benefit from it!

Much depends of course upon the interviewer himself. If he is genuinely seeking valid information for the viewing public he will ask the right questions and the subject, if he is sincere, will make the correct answers. Of course if he is devious and has something to hide, then it *is* up to the questioner to try and get the truth out of him. It is a cut-throat game of silky voices and nerves of double-edged steel, with the ultimate object of a big news scoop or scandal.

That, of course, is in the future. When new to television, like public speaking, you are being seen as well as heard. But on television laymen are often subconsciously confused between the sound and vision aspects. Thus their concentration is split two ways, between appearance and what they are going to say. They have to cope with a great *unseen* audience for the first time.

Thus, subjects often become very self-conscious when first in a studio. They are told not to stare directly at the camera – so their eyes move ceaselessly round looking at *everything else*, the roof, walls, their own hands, the arms of the chair in which they are sitting bolt upright with tension. It is understandable enough, but your public speaking will have taught you repose and, if you can accept the novelty of the situation by being both calm and natural, you will come through it well.

We cannot help being nervous, but the best way to relax is to consider the occasion as a chat or business talk between yourself and one other, to regard the millions viewing merely as an involved third party. You have to be aware that your information is for other ears than the interviewer's, but he is their spokesman.

You cannot go wrong if you make him your focal point for those wandering eyes and, as you ease into the interview, you will soon find yourself acting with composure. Television shows up those who would try to be 'personalities' immediately they are on the screen. Some try too hard to be liked, to come across as 'attractive characters' much as they do in public speaking. But the camera can come into very revealing close-up! Bombasts, would-be funny men, the proud and the prejudiced have to be very good actors indeed to escape the merciless scrutiny of the lens.

It is a sad fact of life that certain public figures have lost out through having a poor television 'image', especially in political fields. Regrettably the world is not yet sufficiently educated in compassion to rise above intolerantly assessing people just by their beauty or their ugliness alone. Once when there were only newspapers and radio reporting to acquaint us in depth with public figures, plus, perhaps, a fleeting glimpse of them on agitated cinema newsreels, their achievements and their thinking were the all-important factors. Now, with television, it takes the plain and homely a long time to gain a rapport with the majority of audiences, and they have to be experienced to do so. A good television image has become a necessity in many walks of life.

Already accomplished public speakers will know to avoid physical fidgeting on television. We have all seen the head wagglers, saying 'yes' but nodding negatively. They jerk their chins forward in emphasising points and, when listening to the questioner, cock their head sideways in rather an arch manner. They over-react to his words, roll eyes, raise or dramatically drop the head, clasp hands, cup chins, point fingers, hunch shoulders like a watchful goal-minder, their smile always knowing and impish. That strange gremlin who takes over certain people appearing on television, prompts them to feel they must move as well as speak in front of cameras. All such gymnastics are most irritating to viewers as they detract from the spoken word. The head must be kept steady, the hands relaxed and resting easily.

Another hazard in early television appearances is catching the interviewer's 'tone'. Nerves cause this as subconsciously the subject imitates the interviewer's timbre, taking it as a sort of tuning fork for the right note and having hit it, stays on that tone the whole time. This impressionable trait is more obvious in television and radio than in other forms of public speaking, although it can happen in that field as well. A beginner has been known to start his speech in complete accord with the loud tones of the toastmaster who has just announced him! It is an instinctive refuge for a new speaker. The sound has just proved acceptable to the audience and he fears his own might be insignificant in comparison. So he continues in the same tone ... which can, inadvertently, sound as if he is mocking the previous speaker!

As more and more commercial concerns are using television as a means of communication, sending recorded and filmed talks abroad or selling ideas or products to clients without any representative having to use a passport, so you will find yourself having to appear on the medium. This will not be mere entertainment in the home; this will be part of your work, your livelihood. Being on television is not just something that impresses the neighbours any more; your future progress could one day depend upon your ease and control in front of cameras.

You may well have to use a fairly basic vocabulary if your audiences are from non-English speaking countries. You have to impress them with the function of your product, not your rhetoric. But it helps, too, if your tie is straight!

Too often television appearances are spoiled by the subjects not doing their research well enough before the programme. They hope it will be all right on the night, that they can get by and will be cool, calm and collected when dealing with off-the-cuff questions. But studio tensions are manifold, you may have to be 'made up' which makes your face feel slightly tighter, you may have to wait a long time before you are called. So by the time your particular green light flickers you can feel very tense indeed.

Then the brain is not so active with ad-libs. So out comes the familiar 'well ... er ... !' 'funny you should ask that ...' (when it is not the least extraordinary!), 'that's a good question ...' all swirling valuable time down the drain. The other time-waster is when the interviewer asks: 'Have you been to Chicago?' and the reply comes: 'Yes, I have been to Chicago ...' More seconds thrown on the scrap heap.

To succeed in vision you must train yourself to be succinct. However sophisticated or erudite you may think long words might be for your 'image identification', you will only really be popular with producers if you can supply more information per ten seconds than the others!

Of course if you graduate into the more educational strata of television with lecture-style programmes, you will have more scope. Mostly your work will be pre-filmed but still be 'timed' to the last line. Watching the clock does not mean gabbling, of course. You still must enunciate clearly but, while keeping your sentence construction entertaining and colourful, you also keep it simple.

Radio

To fill their air time local radio stations depend a great deal upon interviews, not only with celebrities 'passing through', but with residents who are experts in particular fields. The voicing of parochial matters, grievances over community concerns, opinions on council matters and general information concerning an area, find radio a sure way of spreading a gospel or launching a crusade.

The radio microphone is uncannily sharp in accuracy, picking up the slightest hesitancy, the over-drawn breath or even the click of dentures. Unlike the television screen where synchronising vision might help reduce the effect of verbal errors, radio seems to magnify them as there is no compensating factor beyond the ear. If your talk is recorded prior to transmission the producer will explain that, should you make a slip of the tongue or 'fluff' (i.e. miss a syllable or mispronounce a word) you should pause for three seconds, then return to the nearest full stop and start again from there. This allows him space to get the scissors in and rejoin the tape and also gives you the chance to maintain correct tone. Glossing over a word-slip in a 'live' talk often makes it all the more obvious because the hesitation alters fluency and voice pitch.

However few talks of a lengthy nature go out 'live' today. The value of a recording is that it can go on the air any time – and be repeated later – to suit the planners and does not bind them to relying upon the speaker's availability on a specific day. So, once again, time is gold dust.

However interviews are often 'on the spot' so, if you need them, prepare a few notes to assist you while on the air. With a ready-reference to hand, you may well make a few points that the interview could miss.

Radio may seem reasonably uncomplicated, but there is a strange coldness in a studio. Television employs a considerable studio staff so you are surrounded by technicians when you appear, but radio gives you a much more isolated sensation. If you are being interviewed you will see perhaps only your questioner and the controller through a glass panel. When giving a full talk you will be alone in the studio with the producer at the controls through that same panel. He or she will make everything easy for you – but it can, at first, be quite a strange experience. Fortunately the taping of such talks lessens the nervous strain. Once upon a time speakers had to go out 'live' – quite an ordeal when you think of it, as every mistake – and cough – was heard by the listening public!

In a full length talk you will, of course, use a script. This demands a very particular technique. You must avoid it sounding as if it is being read. The fact that it is a script does not mean it should come over as the written word, text-bookish in style. It must be delivered informatively but in a conversational tone. That is why we suggested in speech scripts that you think of them in the form of a letter to a friend. In that way your descriptive style will be free and natural. Much, of course, depends on the subject, but if you can make science sound fun, more people will listen to you.

You will need diligent rehearsal for solo broadcasts, long before you reach the studio. Once the producer has passed the script and you have timed it correctly, you must read it through, time and again, to get the pace, pauses and emphasis right on target. For your own peace of mind you have to stick at it so that, once in that studio to record it, you can more or less do it in one 'take'. To some such long term application is an anathema. Radio producers find too often that many qualified speakers do not readily dedicate themselves to projects involving time out for deep study. Perhaps they feel that shutting themselves away with a script for detailed rehearsal might make them miss some speedily passing band wagon upon which they feel they should jump. The result is they come to the studio ill-prepared and the talk takes hours to record.

Radio is the best medium for really creative thinking. Performers on it produce words designed for listeners to translate into pictures in an entirely personal way, much as public speakers must do. Regular listeners to 'sound' word programmes are inevitably stimulating conversationalists because their minds are geared to formulating individual ideas beyond television which tries to do all the work for them. This is particularly applicable to children who, fed on a television diet, do not develop keen imaginations and perhaps, psychologically, expect life to be equally cut and dried for them.

There is a pressing need for the young to have their creative faculties trained by the effort of 'visualising' the unseen and being creators within themselves rather than slavishly follow trends set by others. Certainly it would improve their public speaking. As a father once said: 'I don't mind my daughter not agreeing with me. It is her inability to explain *why* which bothers me....'

11

Speaking in the Open Air

Audiences with no roof over their head have wandering eyes. Within four walls they are more likely to confine their attention to a speaker on the platform, but *alfresco* functions provide them with additional sights and sounds, trees rocking in a breeze, the sound of passing traffic and a thousand other diversions including feeling cold! Functions such as fêtes, bazaars, charity sports matches, 'bring-and-buy' fairs and exhibitions are tricky events for public speakers.

Our advice is to keep your remarks as brief as possible. Perhaps in political rallies you may be expected to expound more fully but, even then, in a town square, your message should be short, simple, and straightforward for the throng to absorb amid extraneous noise.

At fêtes, your hearers are there primarily to enjoy the swings, roundabouts or whatever else is billed as the attractions. They want to hear raffle prize-winning numbers, bingo callers and see the sights. Frankly they are more interested in what the prizes are than who is presenting them. However famous you may be, they are not prepared to listen to you for more than a few minutes. They want information as to times of events, where the autograph tent is for them to capture celebrities' signatures or the exact location of the beer or tea tent. So your address – it is hardly a speech – should consist of welcoming them, a brief reference to the charity concerned, acknowledgements and thanks to the organisers – then quickly cutting the tape to declare it open, if that is the drill.

Any speaker naive enough to try and use such an occasion for political dogma at any length is asking for trouble. They will not listen for long. If you must make a special point, it is essential to keep it as a pithy, brief insertion into the usual for-malities so that, by its isolated brevity, it sticks in the mind. No good enlarging upon it – make the short statement and then sit down. Any such speech, whether you are a guest of honour opening the proceedings, or a supporting speaker, must be brief and entirely relevant to the occasion.

At some less equipped functions you might be handed only a loud-hailer to make such an address. The distortion that causes is another reason for not prolonging a speech. After a couple of minutes of a loud-hailer peroration, the audience will begin wandering away, equating your sound with airport or railway announcements which do not affect them!

If you do have to speak on such occasions try, if it is pos-sible, to check that your microphone is in first-class order. Such open-air functions are liable to suffer from bad amplification and 'feed-back' into the microphones by badly placed speakers. There may well be insufficient in use so that not every strategic part of the fairground is covered. Thus some members of the public hear you clearly, some only distortedly and others not at all. People who have paid entrance fees do not like this 'favouritism'!

If you do have any control over the organisation, make it your business, before the gates open, to have the sound facili-ties tested all round the area of events. Place helpers at various points, especially on the peripheries of activity, to check that speech can be heard clearly in all parts. Make your testing speech original. Do not just count or recite the alphabet, other-wise, even if a checker hears familiar words distortedly, he may subconsciously think it clear enough for ordinary audibility. Give those checking an entirely new test, with a few longish words so that they will have to listen intently to report back what you have said. Then, if certain parts of the ground are not getting a good reception, you have time to adjust it before the public are admitted.

Nothing is worse for a fund-raising event out-of-doors than poor sound equipment. Too often charity organisations, especially the smaller ones, over-economise on the microphone costs. Money is lost if those supporting the cause cannot hear what is going on. You must have loud and clear communication if you want a generous response.

Check, too, that your sound does not affect people in neighbouring houses. Nothing mars these occasions more than the arrival of a police car in the middle of the afternoon in response to a noise disturbance complaint. If it happens to be a Sunday, the sudden blaring of voice and music across garden fences can, if unexpected, make a lot of people angry.

This can be avoided by a letter to each nearby householder or a personal call from one of your committee members with the exact information as to when the event will open and close so that all concerned are in the picture. Offer them free entrance tickets if need be and treat them as VIPs if necessary. Most people will be entirely agreeable if they feel you have shown the right concern for their welfare before the event gets under way. Even the biggest sports stadiums in the world receive complaints from distracted householders in the vicinity, so take trouble not to make unnecessary enemies. If court action resulted, your funds might suffer heavily. Charity does begin at home.

An individual letter of thanks to them should also follow the event. Possibly have it ready by the time the fête opens so that your star guest can sign it. That will make next year's attempt much easier to organise. Committees should make surrounding householders feel an integral part of the occasion and pay due tribute to their patience and understanding when having to keep their windows closed on a really hot summer's day.

Rallies and demonstrations

Again, despite the policies involved, keep your speeches short. Too many speakers repeat themselves on these occasions. The crowd with their banners know why they are there, so do not harp on the reasons but speak on the future plans. Try not to be content to exhort the crowd with vague good intentions. If you want their support in your fight you must explain the practicalities of exactly how you intend to take up arms for the cause.

Useless oratory is heard far too often at demonstrations.

There are threats of action and loud proclamations of faith and trust – but what your adherents want is a positive programme. They all know the fault – they are there to hear the cure. If you have not got it, you should not be there wasting the time of both the police and the gathered people. Preaching to the converted is easy – giving them practical advice is perhaps more difficult, but that should be your aim.

Open air speaking is best illustrated by a visit to Speaker's Corner in London's Hyde Park. There you will hear sincerity and crankdom, side by side. But you will also witness some magnificently brave speakers ... people who really put themselves on an altar of sacrifice for their beliefs.

Listen, as well, to their vocabulary – and hear how well it suits the open-air.

12

Taking Charge of Public Speaking Occasions

As you progress through various stages of public speaking, social, political, technical, commercial, tutorial, you are likely to be called upon to fill what may be termed 'controlling' roles. A good chairman is vital at meetings of all types. He or she must be experienced in handling audiences as well as follow speakers, must be alert to atmosphere, true to the agenda and direct events both ethically and fairly. A good host or hostess at a private party is a form of chairmanship, for they need the confidence of facing guests and quietly controlling proceedings without being too obviously a director − or worse, a dictator.

Those public speakers who are show business-minded might find themselves master of ceremonies, compères or commeres of entertainments. Societies unable to afford the luxury of a toastmaster often appoint an MC from within their own membership to cover both the announcement of after-dinner speakers and cabaret. Even a bingo caller or disc jockey needs public speaking confidence to perform his specialist job. If you are called upon to take charge of any function, whether for adults or children, you will need to be experienced in facing and handling critical audiences.

Not all good public speakers are necessarily expert controllers of occasions. Many are too extrovert, unable to resist the temptation to use the status in a narrow personalised way. Other good speakers may be too specialised in their particular fields to handle audiences outside them. However, whether for business or pleasure, it will inevitably fall the lot of any practised public speaker to be asked to 'command' an event and, with tactful control, ensure its smooth running.

Chairmanship

First and foremost he or she must be impartial. Only if obliged by articles of association or consent of the meeting, when a chairman has to make a casting vote on important issues, should that impartiality not be observed.

Being appointed chairman does not necessarily make you the star of the occasion. Usually it is the reverse, especially at social functions when celebrity guest speakers are the main attraction. Any chairman who tries to outshine them is ill-fitted for the job. He or she must extend the full courtesies to guests and members alike and, even if prejudiced against particular speakers or, in business meetings, any motion, fair play must be the order of the day. Sincerity is imperative when in control of a gathering and chairmen must be prepared to subordinate their own preferences to give the right balance to an arranged programme.

Often a chairman is the first speaker. He or she sets the tenor of the event, especially being firm that other speakers do not exceed their brief or their allotted time by setting a good example himself. Hence the need for tact. A good chairman who feels a speaker might outstay his welcome can, in his opening address, issue a veiled warning, charmingly put, that time is short and apologise, in advance, for making speakers toe the line. It may not always work with some thick-skinned orators, but at least the audience know the chairman has their interests at heart.

A good chairman must be approachable by all from a dinner waitress to the VIP guest. Too often chairmanship is regarded as an élitist status controlling the occasion undemocratically, making personal rules and advocating individual tastes which are often contrary to the enjoyment of the audience. For example a chairman might belong to some guild or organisation with special traditions and rituals and these he will try and infuse into ordinary social gatherings or works parties. He will be

a poor choice of chairman anyway because he needs set protocol guidelines to exercise control. Chairmen must be able to
improvise and adjust formalities to suit any occasion.

As the lynchpin in a smooth-running function, a chairman
is the main supporting player to the star attractions and he
makes sure that events leading up to their appearance go without a hitch.

Weak chairmen are the bane of functions. They do not ensure
that a social evening's running order or a meeting's agenda is
followed strictly to the letter, but allow liberties to be taken.
Usually they will be lethargic themselves in getting the proceedings under way at the appointed hour. They will either
arrive late themselves or keep their guests far too long in the
bar after the dinner gong has sounded. Thus, they are regarding
the event as their 'personal night' and not as one for the audience. They will disregard realistic and experienced advice from
committee members already used to running such occasions.
Chairman who try to do things 'their' way through self-importance and absolute convenience to themselves can wreck social
occasions, meetings – and even their own careers!

The job is unobtrusive – unless things get out of hand and a
chairman is obliged to take a firm line. And it must be a rock-
hard firm line, not vacillating or fence-sitting. Teamwork must
be ensured so that those who have appointed tasks are allowed
to perform them without hindrance. Many chairmen are often
so carried away with their exalted moment that they will even
bob up and make announcements which should be the responsibility of a toastmaster or master of ceremonies. At board meetings they will dominate by intolerance of other viewpoints, as
well as exhibiting a complete disregard for normal procedure.
One always admires people who can get things done with a
minimum of formality, but this can be dangerous if carried to
extremes by an overbearing personality.

Being a chairman gives you power to control events, but not
necessarily dictate policies. You are not a judge or magistrate,
you are an impartial voice, the meditator or the referee who
must not make his own rules, but interpret those set down by
the occasion.

Chairmanship is not an easy job. It demands great patience and tact – and a sense of humour – to turn heated exchanges into logical discussion, soothe ruffled feelings and yet be ready to take strong action against snide behaviour. The welfare of the cause must be truly within the chairman's heart; he or she must act for the over-all good of the occasion, accept majority verdicts and, above all, be as good a listener as a speaker.

If you are shown to be a weak chairman at the onset, there will be those round the table who are all too ready to take advantage of your indecisive approach. However unethically others on boards or committees may try to behave, a chairman must remain, like the Speaker in the House of Commons, entirely unbiased but possess the full knowledge of the rules governing his post and his decisions.

Few of us are such saints as not to be influenced by certain self-interests but, if we take the chair, we must stick to the truth and nothing but it. Then our decisions, however unpopular with certain factions, cannot be challenged on unethical grounds. Judgements must be made on the objective facts. Difficult members must be considered not on their personalities but by the reasons behind their thinking. Disliking a character does not necessarily mean that the brain children he conceives must be counter-productive.

To be a good chairman is a splendid asset, not only to yourself but to your work, your community and your politics. Sincerity is the key factor once again – and a gentle but unswerving power to command.

Master of ceremonies

A master of ceremonies is not necessarily the mastermind of the function. Normally, he is the one who carries out someone else's plan. However, he is not a compère, although the jobs are not dissimilar. The master of ceremonies, or MC, is really an extension of a toastmaster's job at a lunch or dinner in that he goes further than just announcing speakers and intervals, to linking events together, using a more intimate formula. At seminars and long-running courses, for example, in the business world, a good MC is vital. He or she is the pivotal figure around which all activity swings. The time-table and, more importantly, any changes of syllabus are conveyed to participants by the MC. He must address the classes or meetings before and after lectures and talks. An MC must be prepared for more off-the-cuff announcements than any other in the work force. He is the mouthpiece for the organisers and students alike.

A good MC will not try to be facetious or crack jokes as would a compère on a social evening. The MC's technique is only distantly related to showbusiness, whereas a compère is a blood brother being involved entirely in the presentation of performers in cabaret and on stage. Both might announce dances at a ball, but the compère alone will handle the floor show. That is the difference. An audience expects fun and games from a compère but an MC, while he can still be congenial and amusing, is there to provide information as to the progress of the event.

Firms wishing their seminars and trade exhibitions to be handled concisely with good, precise announcements as to developments taking place, must beware of selecting a man or woman for the job who will turn it into a highly-personalised compère role.

An MC must liaise with all the organising officials before a function and on the day have in his head a clear running order of events. He must know all officials and their separate roles while keeping close contact with everyone behind the scenes. They, in turn, must inform the MC of any late changes or new developments affecting the schedule. This avoids the chairman being harried by several officials at once all making late changes. It is up to the MC to inform the chairman of alterations, so that he is not thrown by any surprise element. The MC has his finger on the pulse of the whole event and co-ordinates each item. An efficient MC is of inestimable value and many companies train personnel especially for this important job.

Women are often better equipped for it than men. They can command a more chivalrous respect from an audience than can men and often, when already experienced in office work, possess a far greater sense of responsibility.

Someone likely to take a few drinks during the proceedings is not advocated, however strong a head an MC has for alcohol. The MC must always be 'in the wings' so to speak, readily available to smooth out a sudden crisis or fill a lull in the proceedings, be able to make ad lib announcements without having to make notes first, besides taking important last-minute decisions almost in full view of the audience.

Where the MC and compère's job overlaps is in keeping the pace of the event going and avoiding long pauses which create boredom. If a lecturer is to address a 'class' the MC must ensure the students are in their seats before announcing him. A lot of MC work is done in corridors, herding up lost sheep and infusing a sense of discipline necessary to the occasion.

'Mastering a Ceremony' is harder work than the light-hearted bonhomie of compèring and also less rewarding from an audience's appreciation viewpoint. Any company or society, however, which has a good MC at their disposal is extremely fortunate.

Some chairmen like to combine their job with that of MC but, if they are wise, they will appoint an aide to tackle the latter role to work closely with him but leave him free to make his own contribution from the chair more outstanding. During a protracted event a chairman who has been bouncing up and down making extraneous, run-of-the-mill announcements loses the vital element of novelty when he rises to make his own speech. By that time the audience will have already heard a good deal from him, his voice become too familiar so vital impact is lost at his big moment.

Being an MC is a splendid exercise for anyone keen on public speaking. You have contact with audiences and will experience backstage preparation in making a function operate smoothly. You will employ economy of phrasing, understand timing and pace – and you must have good diction to be so selected.

Compères

... do not necessarily have to be good speech-makers – indeed very few are – but they do require a certain pleasing audacity in public. Their job is to link stage acts of all kinds and, at the same time, keep the audience cheerful while they maintain the programme at a good pace. The professional may, for example, have to patter away at some length while, backstage, apparatus is erected for a wire-walking act or a grand piano is moved into place. Knowing the running-order of the programme he will keep the audience amused until he gets a signal from the wings that all is ready for him to announce the next turn.

Sometimes the amateur will take too long telling involved stories instead of 'quickies' and become so carried away that he will take up more time than the act he is introducing. Also he may indulge in the 'crime' of telling funny stories before a comedian comes on. That sort of one-upmanship, often the ploy of a veteran compère when heralding a newcomer to the business, is two-edged. If the audience are eagerly awaiting the comic's appearance they will not give full ear to a rambling compère. When announcing any star attraction a compère is advised to keep his introduction brief, otherwise he is not only wasting his own valuable material but holding up the proceedings.

Some would-be comedians see compèring as an easy way to raise laughter, just popping on and off cracking jokes with time in the wings to refresh his memory from a notebook instead of having to learn and rehearse a full act. The job, of course, is far more subtle than that. A compère is the link man and, like a public speaker, must be completely involved with the show in spirit, not an individual doing a succession of isolated acts between all the others.

The audience must be made to feel the compère is their representative on stage. He has to strike a happy medium being part of backstage and front-of-the-house. Identifying himself too much with the artists in the wings, can, unless they are really big stars themselves, make an audience feel remote and at arm's length from the show. Such compères get a relatively unresponsive reception which can undermine the other acts on the bill.

Compères have direct communication with an audience which some other acts may not have, such as purely visual artists, acrobats and dancers, so they have to engender a warmth between them and the audience, enthuse in their announcements as the personal contact between both sides of the curtain. A sign of a practised compère is when he uses 'we' instead of 'you', in addressing an audience. The first person plural means that they are completely involved with the audience, the second person leaves only an impression of detachment.

As in public speaking a compère has to be deeply concerned with time. If a show is over-running he must cut his own patter. If there are backstage hold-ups he must increase it, holding the fort until things are put right. On stage, too, he must ensure that if the act he is presenting needs to use his same microphone, he leaves it in the right place for them. How often do we see a girl singer in an amateur show come on stage to find the microphone too far back and its head towering over her own, left by a six foot compère. A compère has the responsibility of presenting artists to their fullest effect.

A compère's style depends upon his stage personality, of course, Many otherwise talented stars are not always good compères as their delivery is too personalised for straight announcements. Their inbred staccato or drawling diction may not always blend with the fluency required for linking a whole show. Many try compèring but only a small percentage really succeed in making the job their full-time career. It does involve an adjustment to circumstances which not all comedians are prepared to make. Any show in which a compère gives obvious signs of 'competing' with the other acts on the bill will suffer from lack of balance.

Compèring for the amateur looks easy – but it demands great skill and a strong sense of teamwork. A compère must be considerate, entirely professional in outlook yet, when needs be, self-effacing. The transition from being public speaker to compère is far simpler than the reverse process. Showbusiness audiences are far less demanding in that they know exactly what to expect when they tip down their seats.

13

Audiences and Critics

Throughout this book audience reaction is mentioned in almost every aspect of public speaking. At first beginners are apt to give them only secondary concern but, beyond the obvious objective of any public speaker to satisfy audiences, there is another aspect, that of assessing them. As you gain proficiency in speaking you will discover you have gained a certain perception in audience format, an intuitive analysis of the people you are to address.

If, when you rise, you are following other speakers you will have already judged the audience's main characteristic – eager, enthusiastic, apathetic, casual, uninterested, frigid, intolerant or over-burdened with drunks! Previous speakers have suffered or enjoyed speaking to them. Speaking later you have a chance either to capitalise on their success or endeavour to offset their failure by tackling such a disappointing audience in another way. You will find this challenge occurring many times in your speaking career. With better material, better timing and a more suitable approach than the others, you may well lift a dull crowd beyond just the applause of relief that, at last, someone knows their job, to very real appreciation for a speaker who is both entertaining and interesting and therefore right up their street.

Since medieval court jesters were beheaded for unapproved jokes, the enigma that is an audience has baffled all those who appear in public. Actors touring in a play have found it well received in Edinburgh, hated in Glasgow, popular in Manchester, a failure in London. The performances have not varied to any violent degree, the plot has not altered – yet still the cast has to face divergent criticism. Theatre managements are permanently perplexed by quixotic audience reactions.

What makes an audience? A group of people gather together, most of whom are strangers to each other – and yet form into one characteristic mass. Despite the thousands of differences in each member's metabolism, one specific accord is reached *in toto*. Despite obvious degrees and shades of individual opinion, they fuse to be either keen to enjoy your speech, or cold which makes your effort a chore. Altering their demeanour midstream is difficult, but it can be done and the cold turned to warmth because a new and more attractive influence which suits their mental state has worked upon them. Unfortunately the reverse can happen and one poor speaker spoil the good work which has gone before.

In public speaking you stand or fall by your audience. Some thick-hided speakers may drone on for years oblivious of the fact they bore their audiences to distraction, but the really sensitive will struggle hard to correct and adjust their particular approach. Soon, then, they inherit that sixth sense of assessment, an impulse which tells them to omit certain passages for specific audiences, or where to insert special additions exclusive to one particular section of the community.

Beginners have the disadvantage of usually being first to appear on a bill of speakers, always a tough, demanding proposition. However, it is logical. Organisers have to balance their speakers to ensure the beginning does not outweigh the end. They will put their star attraction last to make certain, at least, the audience will go home pleased. Naturally they will not risk inexperience to close an evening. Learners must understand this and be prepared to gain experience the hard way.

Of course it has happened, if only rarely, that the first speaker, an unknown newcomer, has shown such brilliance and flair that he or she becomes hard to follow. That is good for public speaking, because the more such challenges the old hands have to face, the less likely they are to take their practised expertise as gospel. In public speaking you never stop learning.

The vagaries of audiences mean that there can never be a definable perfection-peak in speech making. That, too, is all to the good. Like athletes, speakers cannot always expect to win

but, at least, they can go on giving continually good performances. But you will not if you disregard audiences. Even *en
masse* every person amongst them thinks himself important. It
is a natural reaction. There will be some who admire your
talent, others envious of it. Certain individuals play hard to get
and have to be wooed before you can win them over. Some
may be there under some sort of duress and will stubbornly
refuse to accept whatever is offered. Others will go determined
to enjoy themselves. Audiences are composed of the interested,
the disinterested and the uninterested and much depends upon
the majority category in each gathering. A predominance of
'interested' parties will sway the whole if the speakers are good
but, if they are low standard, the other two factions will say 'I
told you so'.

You will notice this particularly when you have hit upon a
successful speech which you make many times. It takes you
round the country always, it seems, proving infallible and the
applause constantly rings out in your honour. Then, suddenly
without apparent justification, one day the appreciation graph
unaccountably drops and, despite past triumphs, prompts only
a tepid reception. Puzzled, you ask yourself why. The audience
seemed the usual type, much like those who applauded you in
recent weeks. Yet this particular lot were only semi-enthusi-
astic, their manner stiff and the handclaps seemingly only
polite.

Yet, at the reception afterwards, you may well be congratu-
lated upon the best speech they have heard that session! The
audience in that case will possibly consist of a society membership, an entirely reserved body of people, alike in characteristic
because of their club's constitution. For once the composition
of the assembly was one of more or less total integration of like
temperaments and interests which formed an undemonstrative
whole. Then you would have your reason for their seemingly
detached interest. Some people are shy of showing their feelings
unguardedly among those with whom they share a large part of
their lives. Individually they might tell you they enjoyed your
work afterwards, but would not want to lose their statuesque
front in an audience!

Thus you will find many societies, ladies' luncheon clubs, all-male rotary and other organisations where specific membership qualification is a particular common interest, often band to-gether to form one prevailing mood. They are a challenge to any speaker, can be unassailable brick walls or so receptive that, in anticipation of laughter to come, they may even chuckle when you begin 'Ladies and gentlemen'. These latter, rare though they are, do restore your faith in human nature. They will give you a standing ovation, you will feel on top of the world – but re-member that they will not necessarily represent your next audience!

The sports club audience are predictably jocular and take liberties with a speaker, possibly with good-natured heckling or hearty 'hear hears', all determined somehow to get into the act. Speakers invited to address them are usually cast in the right mould. No one expects a solemn speech on such occasions un-less concerned with the technicalities of a particular game. Laughter is the order of the day, plus, perhaps, one pedestrian speech on matters of club policy. And no speaker in his right mind would try and rally political support or soberly attempt to academically educate such an audience!

Audiences consisting of mainly one sex do give you some obvious clues as to how to make your talk appealing. Organ-isers will book you because your subject interests them. If you are already on the speaking circuits your reputation will have gone ahead of you so that, in this field, you should never find yourself facing an entirely inappropriate audience.

It is the 'general public' audiences which remain the most unpredictable. We cited theatre examples earlier. What makes them jell into one lump of discontent or effervesce like spark-ling champagne? There may be circumstances mitigating their mood. Heavy rain soaking them before they reach the venue, a transport strike, a cold hall, bad box office organisation, a poor meal at a dinner or a hundred and one other obstacles to enjoy-ment hours before you stand up. Lecturers in Britain often speak of the deadly effect of snow on their audiences – but find it no handicap whatsoever in Canada when audiences travel hun-dreds of miles through it to hear them. It is all relative to local conditions. If there are 'debit side' circumstances on the day of your talk, they may well affect your audience's concentration.

This state of affairs is no help, but unfortunately audiences are your barometer of success and failure. You will still be expected to lift them from any gloom and despondency an act of God or human error has caused. If you are aware of what it is, then mention it, thank them in advance for braving the elements or putting up with administrative inconveniences to hear you. If you can think up a suitable anecdote, tell them how you, also, have been personally affected by it. Become involved in their problem, reach out and join them right at the beginning of your talk. Once they realise that you are capable of such spontaneity you will be surprised how they will warm to you. Subconsciously they will say to themselves 'here is a speaker who is considerate' and you should be able to restore the balance.

Every experienced speaker knows it is useless to blame an audience for failure, but many still try! Certainly if he or she has an agent who later informs them of the true unlucky background to a poor reception, it will not be held against the speaker. However, the agent would much prefer to hear that the speaker he booked for a function received a rapturous ovation from an audience, most of whom have been in a train accident on their way to hear him!

You will never please all the audiences you face, but the pendulum will swing more towards enthusiasm and even higher acclaim if you always maintain a steadfast standard of speaking. Few audiences are unaware of diligence and will take that into consideration even if they find the subject or personality of a speaker not quite as they would desire. It is speakers who, in their opinion, take liberties which annoy them, while those who try too hard to be liked always make them suspicious. As you do the speaking rounds you will hear of extroverts who are either loved or hated by various audiences. Because of their perhaps outlandish approach, there can be no half measure of appreciation – they are either considered terrible or marvellous. These types of speakers know this and stoically take the rough with the smooth, but most want to widen their audiences and so begin to tone their talks down.

There are those who find young audiences hard to please because they rely too much on nostalgia in their talks which is only adored by more mature citizens. Later experience teaches such speakers to select their venues and only appear where they are certain there is common ground. Young speakers often suffer the reverse problem, a criticism being that some of them do not respect older people's preferences and are constantly mocking them. Certainly there should not be any obvious generation gap in public speaking. For a cause to be entirely successful it has to appeal to all age-groups.

You cannot speak without audiences and, irrational as they sometimes seem, they make or break you. That is why we stressed them so much in the plotting and delivery of your talks. We repeat that too many speakers prepare speeches entirely for their own vanity and, if the truth be known, never once think that the audience might not accept their words or their demeanour. Audiences are rarely captive enough to sit through being bored or affronted. They must be borne in mind when you write and rehearse a speech.

However complicated their reactions, often infuriatingly obtuse and stubborn, there are few entirely unsympathetic audiences outside the political arena. The safest method of pleasing them is to be yourself, affect no poses nor elevate yourself beyond your true level. Audiences resent being 'conned' or patronised. They want to feel involved, of course, and if they sense an empathy, an understanding in your speech, plus a spirit which they appreciate, they will lean forward intently.

Criticism

The public speaking world is full of listeners who feel they could do better. The majority would fail if the chips were down and they had to face an audience, and the ambitious who have failed will denigrate those who have made the grade.

In your speaking career you will meet such critics. Some you will immediately spot as being transparently jealous of your success. They will pick holes in one solitary aspect of your speech, or complain that an anecdote you used was very old. If the audience has laughed and really enjoyed it, then there is your answer. In fact, whenever criticism is launched at you concerning your material, if you have evidence that those hearing you fully appreciated the point, that is an incontrovertible reply to critics.

What hurts most, of course, is valid criticism. Someone hits upon a weakness which you know, within yourself, to be a fact but hoped you had masked skilfully. It is infuriating when a critic finds real chinks in your armour. However try, if you can, to bite back that first curt denial, pause and take stock – then admit it. Mostly a critic facing you with such observations has the answers, otherwise he would not button-hole you in the first place. So ask him exactly what you should do about the defect. If he is exercising some sort of one-upmanship he will be taken aback – but if really genuine he will tell you the truth.

No one is the worse for being wiser. Take all the advice you can. Some will be merely flighty, trivial comment, but always along the line you will meet some experienced speaker sitting in the body of the hall who knows exactly your feelings as you rise to speak. If they proffer personal advice never be afraid to take it.

One criticism, though, is irrevocable. However much you might justify your speech's appeal to the audience, if you have spoken too long, your critics are right. No good your insisting that you were not boring; the censorship that you 'stole' other speakers' time is valid. Never lay yourself open to this charge.

Perhaps through television with its surfeit of speakers of all styles appearing in the home, people are now prone to criticise more than congratulate. It is an age of comparison. Critics unable to really pin-point a lucid criticism will tell you flatly that you were not as good as the speaker at their last function. They will not enlarge on it, just make that bald statement. There may be many reasons for their overbearing attitude. Perhaps they thought the other speaker more academic or funnier than you.

What you have to assess from such loose, unconstructive observations is – am I rating myself a bit too highly? Why didn't I appeal to that person, however shallow I found him to be?

Any criticism however trumpery, rude or snide, can have a grain of truth somewhere. Obviously you can detect the arrogance of someone whose nose is out of joint by your success. It is difficult to give their comments credence – yet they have gone out of their way to criticise you. Why? Jealousy at the applause you have engendered is probably the cause. Somehow you have snatched his limelight ... he resents it and mollifies himself by a carping criticism.

Yet even that has a value. Not at first perhaps, but in the future. When you have been round the circuits successfully for many years, will you be tempted to mete out harsh criticism to a youngster who has just stolen your honours on a public occasion? Think hard on it. It happens all along the line. Suddenly after a long period of acclamation and big reputation which you have never failed to uphold, comes the David to your Goliath. He or she brings the house down with a brilliant speech. When you rise you know the audience has been swept off its feet already. You still feel equal to the occasion, but this jarring experience has slightly thrown your personality. There is a slight tension in that sudden sense of rivalry.

Do not on any account disregard that good speech and speak on as if 'it had not happened. It has and the audience is still agog with it. So congratulate the speaker, bring your own feelings to the front, even admit that he or she is going to be hard for you to follow. That magnanimous approach wins friends. The audience appreciates that you are in accord with their view of that young person's contribution. Immediately the evening no longer becomes a tourney of who is best, but a team of good speakers. Then you will undoubtedly acquit yourself well even if afterwards you still hear nothing but praise for the sudden-found young 'star'.

If and when that happens recall the time when you were young and once outspoke a VIP. For public speaking to continue in high standard, each 'star' must be superseded by younger 'stars'. You must be glad that the tradition is being carried on – and grateful that even when temporarily so deposed, you are still in the top flight!

Public speaking is personal only in so far as you stand solo to perform it. Once you enter the lists seriously you must accept criticism, challenges and even perhaps direct opposition depending, of course, on the sectors in which you speak. As a lecturer you will not meet your 'rivals' but at dinners and similar functions involving more than one speaker, your paths will cross with many popular and 'hard to follow' fellow guests. Criticism is closely linked with such rivalry, human nature being what it is, but still listen to it.

After all, as a public speaker yourself, criticism will be an integral part of your own stock-in-trade – so you must also be prepared to accept it!

14

Weddings, Anniversaries and other Special Occasions

Your speech for a special occasion must be *special*! It is not a time to refurbish previous speeches in the hope they will fit. If you rise to speak in praise of honoured guests you must pay full tribute.

Unfortunately weddings are often spoiled by 'comedian' speakers who upset the serenity of the event by bawdy jokes about future babies or, far worse, snide references to the honeymoon night. While 'permissiveness' has come to stay, the term is constantly over-generalised as an excuse for low-standard speaking. A wedding is a very personalised affair not only for the bride and groom but also their families. Yet many a self-styled comic uses the occasion as a mere backcloth for his 'act' and so puts the mockers on the occasion. A wedding is not the venue for a sleazy club act, yet the nudge-nudge, wink-wink approach of a best man forcing his questionable jokes on the assembled guests is heard too often. Marriage is a serious step in life for the new husband and wife, and perhaps an occasion of some sadness for their families in the inevitable changes it involves. Good humour there must be in speeches on this auspicious day, but speakers must put the event first and their own personalities a long way second.

Experienced speakers can of course fuse the two, giving the speech an individual treatment peculiar to themselves but still remaining within the context of their brief. This they will do without offence or contrived tangents to crack irrelevant jokes. When you are asked to make a 'special occasion' speech always remember that it is up to you to communicate the importance of the event, not your own.

Of course no one wants a long sonorous discourse of un-relieved praise of the participants. Light relief can be included but never personalise questionable jokes against honoured guests. Any examples which illustrate their ability, ingenuity, humanity or ready wit is good material, but you are not on your feet to score a personal speaking triumph at their expense. Your job is to maintain and, if possible, enhance the dignity of the occasion, not degenerate it by off-beat tactics.

Humour is always a danger. Not all human beings possess the same sense of fun. Even on a special occasion you still have to please the audience. They, more than most, have a stake in the occasion, especially at weddings and family anniversaries, so a speaker who over-reaches himself can bring wrath rather than disdain about his ears. If your task is to propose the health of the happy couple, a hero of the hour, a long-serving employee facing retirement, it is common sense to treat the occasion with the dignity it deserves. In other words any laughs you raise must be of a non-shockable nature. This is not being old-fash-ioned; you will be maintaining your reputation as a speaker for all seasons. You will not be asked again if you let down an event by lack of appreciation of its importance to those directly concerned.

Unless you are a last-minute substitution never make such a speech off the cuff. Many well-intentioned (and perhaps well-wined) speakers have failed when endeavouring to be funny without preparation for such assignments. Not content, as they should be, with a short and sweet contribution, they blunder into the realms of 'Have you heard the one about . . .?' regard-less of its point to the assigned brief. If pressed into service at the eleventh hour say only the right things and sit down! Your speech may not be earth-shattering but it is better than being remembered for upsetting the tenor of the occasion by your vanity.

Special speeches need very careful planning. You must bear in mind constantly that you have a duty to perform which has certain conventions attached to it. You may well be able to carry it out in your own inimitable way, but you still have to please an audience who will expect a certain conformity. Certainly your skill will be remarked upon if you cover the necessary niceties in a neat, witty style, but in order to achieve this you must first put yourself in the seat of the guest you are honouring and to whom you will be primarily addressing your remarks. Avoid even a private joke that he might understand but the rest of the room will not. Veto any references which might be funny in other circumstances but could be misconstrued on a special occasion. Better be safe than sorry in such cases. Never be guilty of 'sending up' events which are deeply important to others on such delicate occasions. When dealing with birthdays, engagement parties, weddings or farewell parties base your preparation on 'good wishes for the future'. Keep that central theme and you will not go far wrong.

15
Summary

This book is unique in the Teach Yourself series because the dexterity of accomplishment depends almost entirely upon the character and personality of the student. Unlike other subjects with set formats of execution, in public speaking there can be no acknowledged peak of over-all perfection, no full marks for a final exam. The only attainment possible is your own highest standard. Once you are accepted by the vast majority of your audiences you will have reached that goal.

Even then, when proficient, you will still continue to learn as the progress of world events dictate the need for new looks into application and presentation. Successful speakers have to be adaptable. As an already skilled motorist handles a new car, testing strange gears and gadgets, so a good speaker will adjust to new subjects, situations and audience outlooks.

There is however a restless impatience among some to seek short cuts in mastering a craft. Vital factors therefore are omitted. There are really no short cuts in public speaking. You need the initial nerve, poise, voice, material and timing to deliver your information. You cannot skate round these vital ingredients, and improvement will only come along the road of experience. Trying to cut corners will lead you into some treacherous public speaking minefields through ignorance of full scholarship.

Where new students become confused is in equating the speed of modern times with an equivalent condensing of instruction. The two are not synonymous – indeed the faster the world revolves the more intricate must be our learning to steady it. The public speaker must be well informed on the task itself before communicating successfully with others. Time factors

have stunted once popular 'eloquence' and older speakers sometimes find adjustment to stop-watch precision difficult to master.
Speeches are not listened to as in past decades with the pleasure
of oral magnificence included as an important adjunct to the
information imparted. Your motto must be 'Let thy speech be
short, comprehending much in a few words'.

The problem is to strike the happy medium between being
too abrupt and boringly long-winded. Old-time orators had to
contend with much 'peasant' simplicity in their audiences.
Devious statesmen blinded them with the obtuse verbiage, but
realists, anxious for votes, spoke extensively in order to get their
message through some thick skulls of the period. Sadly today
some still exist.

In political speaking, when you are anxious to be succinct
and brief you may find it hampering that so many of your
audience do not know the true facts. So you must first put them
in the picture with some sort of preamble because they read no
newspapers and only assimilate half-heard radio and television
news. News in print can be re-read many times to check validity
but broadcast items, with viewers talking to each other during
bulletins, become easily misconstrued – yet later quoted as
true! Thus misconceptions arise in the public mind.

It is imperative that you keep abreast or, if you are skilled,
even ahead of the times. Ageing politicians sadly resort to hoary
arguments in favour of their more vital youth to substantiate
policies simply because the speed of progress leaves them short
on time for research.

Use of the 'past' to indicate flaws on the 'present' is an
ancient part of speech construction. No one can deny its value
but so much depends on the evidence used and in what context.
Pure nostalgia for a lost quietude, slower pace and more neigh-
bourliness is valueless to listeners who did not live in those
times and only think of them in terms of unrelieved Dickensian
squalor.

Yes, you have seemingly to pour quarts into pint pots in your
speaking time. So much to say, so little time to say it. But beware over-using speed at the expense of clear speaking. We hear
it daily on television. 'You were quoted as saying ...' says the

interviewer to the politician, 'Ah' he amends, 'when I said that, what I really meant....' This is the result of woolly speech-making in the first place, the badly-handled phrase, the lack of exactly the right vocabulary to pin-point true intent.

Once you allow yourself to use 'wattle' for 'what will ...' 'gunner' for 'going to ...', 'ennit' for 'isn't it ...' even 'Chews-day' for 'Tuesday' ... you set yourself a lazy pattern. One can say these examples do not matter, that we know what a bad an-nouncer means when he slurs 'ternight' – but it creates a terrible precedent for habitual word and diction slackness which must, one day, land speakers in dire trouble through misinterpretation in matters of world magnitude. A brain merely content to re-main so constantly out of step with its voice must be a danger to those with whom it communicates.

Doubtless as you pursue your speaking interests you have come across the gimmicky 'U' and 'Non U' fads. Literary cliques enjoy them as a sort of class distinction between semi- and fully educated people. When Nancy Mitford began it in 1953 one felt it was designed to put us off the language altogether and, al-though her waspish tongue was in her cheek, it did seem to promote an élitism among those whose profession was words. Mainly it is thoroughly contrived and basically snobbish, as when it insists on one term being more admissable to 'society' than another, e.g. 'lavatory' for 'toilet', 'raincoat' for 'macin-tosh', 'lounge' for 'sitting room', etc. None of these variations are of the slightest importance so long as what you say is clearly understood by everyone.

However, these literary isolationists are justified when they advocate correct pronunciation and true meanings of words. Many language manglers arrogate that, provided a person is understood, it matters little how he or she phrases or constructs a speech. It sounds logical but does an audience have any con-fidence in such a lazy speaker? Does the message have full im-pact? Is there any advantage in blemished speech? What must be the overriding consideration is the irrefutable fact that cor-rect speech leaves no margin for error or misinterpretation.

The biggest humbug in defence of bad speaking is made solely to cover indolent learning. Many speakers who have long overcome initial nervousness still speak hesitantly because their minds have remained untrained to plan their words ahead incisively. Too many such speakers are content to put up with a second-rate presentation of their, to them, first-rate causes, alienating many possible followers by casual, take-it-or-leave-it approach. They may argue that their methods are sincere – but if that were the case, their sincerity would surely cause them to give themselves the best chance by learning clear diction.

Sincerity in public speaking is a key factor but conversely, it is rarely possible to achieve in its one hundred per cent 'holy' definition. Every public speaker knows that there are certain necessary ruses and subterfuges justified by circumstances which if *not* used would actually constitute a form of *insincerity*. In the same way that you would not tell a neighbour bluntly that her husband has been killed in an accident but would try and tenderise the tragedy by a compassionate approach, so there are, in public speaking, certain cases when it is humane to sugar the pill to put your hearers in the right mood to receive the news. It is more sincere to bend a rule or two for the audience's good if the alternative is a stark statement of hard fact which is certain to cause unhappiness. Sincerity is also a genuine concern to ease burdens.

Admittedly the white lie could be said by rigid pundits to be insincere but in public speaking the old adage that the truth never hurt anyone is occasionally a downright lie! When innocent people can be mortally hurt or disillusioned, you have a right to use words of comfort, even of optimism, giving them some slender hope which you know, within yourself, is unlikely to be realised. Of course the truth must be told if withholding it is detrimental to life, limb or the law but there are always compromising, compassionate ways of approaching it.

Time has moved on since, for example, illegitimacy was a 'truth' that must be revealed so that the child victim grew up in deprivation under its constant shadow, rarely to prosper in life for a 'sin' not his own. We know now with more enlightened thinking that there must be a necessary tolerance and our sincerity in handling it will be in the tactful rather than the bombshell approach.

If truth is told merely for spite, to harm when no harm is relevant, then a sincere person will not tell it. Even so they still may not alter it to a lie but mostly just avoid the mention. Sincerity is the use of unspoken pardon, acceptance of human fallibility. In public speaking it is the resolve to be honest in use of fact and advantage and even to under-state a lapse which can affect no one but the unfortunate person concerned.

Private lives are far too often public property these days, an insidious weapon, the professional foul used by out-manoeuvred players in vengeance because they could not match an opponent's skill. Never in your speaking indulge in any smear campaign. Alas it is rife in politics and commercial fields. Humbug, self-righteous indignation and posturing play far too great a part in world utterance. The public are now aware of it and respect for leaders in all realms is lower than ever before in history.

No one of course can lead a wholly unblemished life in this modern age without shutting themselves away in a saintly cell. Even then they would be regarded as selfish in opting out and not getting about to help others!

We make these comments so that when you next listen to speeches, you may find some analytical use for them. It will help you to think *behind* speaker's words and into their motives, study their demeanour, hear their cadence and judge sincerity. Will you be at once suspicious of their intention, is there a depth of compassion in their arguments, are they pompous, illogical or plain power-hungry? Will they be covering jealousy or personal greed? Once at the turn of the century public speakers could hide much insincerity under a brilliance of oratory and old Father Time disturbed them not at all. Now his grandson, the Stop Watch, has opened up a new challenge to speakers to compress their oratory. Millions more hear their speeches into the bargain and if they are not lucid in their statements, they can be cut off with their mouths still open.

A high standard of public speaking must be maintained. Many professionals have expertise, flair, together with other components which help them stimulate audiences but still only a few possess that main ingredient – 'spirit'. Intangible though it is, when a speaker possesses it, it shines through and audiences subconsciously recognise it. Beyond all the facts, figures, information, education and comedy there is that extra fusion of 'true intent'.

You will never know whether or not you possess that 'spirit' because it cannot be learned or contrived. Like 'love' it has many connotations but there is only one that is complete in itself. However, if you bear in mind that your freedom of expression must encompass every man's freedom, you will be well on the way to being a fine public speaker. We know you have the stamina for it because you have reached the end of this book.

We wish you a highly successful speaking career and that your audiences find that elusive 'spirit' glowing through *your* words. Let us hope people will apply to you the same epigram with which Samuel Rogers described Lord Dudley in the nineteenth century ... 'He has a heart, and he gets his speeches from it'.

Appendix

Forms of address for persons of rank

A ruling sovereign: Your Majesty
Members of Royal Family: Your Royal Highness (or plural if more than one present)
Dukes: My Lord Duke
Marquis: My Lord Marquis
Other titles covered by 'My Lord' and 'My Lady'
Presidents: Mr President (also Mr Vice President)
Prime Minister: Mr Prime Minister or Prime Minister
Chancellors in Government: Chancellor (also Madam Chancellor)
Archbishops: Your Grace
Bishop: My Lord Bishop
Doctor of Divinity: Reverend Sir
Dean: Very Reverend Sir
Archdeacon: Venerable Sir
(Clergy with titles can be addressed as 'My Lords')
Lord Chief Justice: My Lord Chief Justice
Other titled judges as 'My Lord'
Ambassadors: Your Excellency
Governors: Your Excellency
Envoys and Chargés d'Affaires: 'Excellency' but this is a courtesy title only
Lord Mayor: My Lord Mayor
Mayors: Mr Mayor (or Madam Mayor)

Forms of address are to be studied in two categories: *(a)* when you are merely including them in your opening address as normal courtesy or *(b)* if you wish to single one particular

VIP out if, for example, you are replying to a speech by him or her. Under *(a)* the lesser titles can be covered under 'My Lords, Ladies and Gentlemen'. Under *(b)* if you are replying to, say, an alderman, you would say: 'Mr Chairman, Alderman Smith, my Lords, ladies and gentlemen' (if peers are present) or just plain, 'ladies and gentlemen', if not.

Always address the 'chair' first. It may well be the President of an organisation holding that office, in which case you will begin 'Mr President, ladies and gentlemen'.

If an exceptional guest of honour is present then you would include him or her in your opening address: 'Mr Chairman (or President or Lord Mayor if he should be presiding), Your Royal Highness (or plural if more than one or a husband and wife), Alderman Smith, My Lords, Ladies and gentlemen'.

Should the chair be taken by a person of rank he could become My Lord Chairman or My Lady President.

Service ranks should only be mentioned if you are replying to, say, a General, Admiral or Air Marshal, etc. down the grades, in person, following their speech.

There can, of course, be countless variations on modes of address according to who is present. Masonic Lodges and other societies have their own forms which will come under each particular instruction.

Once the full title has been given in an opening address it is usual to say 'sir' or 'madam' when referring to them again during your speech.

Knighthoods do not come under 'My Lords, ladies and gentlemen' but the plain 'Ladies and gentlemen' unless a knight has to be singled out when responding to him, when the opening address would be 'Mr Chairman, Sir Trevor Evans, ladies and gentlemen. . . .'

However always check with the organising secretary if you are in any doubt as to form of address or have a word with the toastmaster. Many conventions are dying out and there is a general cutting down of formality in ordinary functions today. However if such courtesies are expected then put them into effect.

Index